# Modes in Dényá Discourse

SUMMER INSTITUTE OF LINGUISTICS

PUBLICATIONS IN LINGUISTICS

Publication Number 79

# Modes in Dényá Discourse

## SAMSON NEGBO ABANGMA

A Publication of
**THE SUMMER INSTITUTE OF LINGUISTICS**
and
**THE UNIVERSITY OF TEXAS AT ARLINGTON**
**1987**

# Contents

# Acknowledgments

This work is based on the thesis presented in partial fulfillment of the requirements for a "doctorat de 3ème cycle" which was defended in the University of Yaoundé October 8, 1981.

I accept full responsibility for the views and material presented here. I am, however, indebted to many people for help, and I wish to express my gratitude to the following especially:

To my supervisor, Dr. Ursula Wiesemann, for her patient guidance, helpful advice, and constant interest in the work. The books and documents she placed at my disposal and her courses in discourse analysis opened my eyes to new and exciting areas of research in linguistics. For this I owe her many thanks.

To the staff of the Department of Linguistics and African Languages at the University of Yaoundé, I am grateful for my initiation into African linguistics and related fields. In particular I am indebted to Dr. Emmanuel Chia who read the first draft and helped me in the initial development of the work.

To my mother, a speaker of Anyang, and to other sources I am deeply indepted for the data used in this study.

To the Société Internationale de Linguistique (SIL), Cameroon-Chad Branch and its director, I am grateful for the privilege of using the SIL library, without which this work could not have been possible.

I am grateful to many friends and colleagues for suggestions and practical assistance along the way: To Dr. John Watters for his suggestions on the verb forms. To Joseph Mfonyam for discussing the work with me several times and giving me helpful suggestions. To Abraham Tanyi and to Agbotar Lucas for their painstakingly typed drafts of the thesis upon which the present work is based. To the Rt. Hon. E. T. Egbe for the material assistance given for the preliminary and final typing of the thesis. And finally, to the editors who spent many hours preparing the manuscript for publication.

To my wife I am particularly grateful for her ceaseless encouragement and moral support, and to my children for love while being deprived of my presence and careful attention during the period of writing.

To God Almighty, for the gifts of insight, perseverance, and good health without which the results of the research would never have seen light.

# Abbreviations and Symbols

| | |
|---|---|
| Attr | Attributive |
| Aud | Audience |
| C | Consonant |
| Cond | Conditional |
| CVS | Complex verb stem |
| Eq | Equative |
| exp | Exposition |
| foc | Focus marker |
| fur | Future |
| Hab | Habitual |
| Hort | Hortative |
| Imp | Imperative |
| ImpAnyt | Anytime imperative |
| ImpImm | Immediate imperative |
| ImpNeg | Negative imperative |
| Incep | Inceptive |
| Indef | Indefinite marker |
| Insistimm | Immediate insistent |
| Nar | Narrator |
| Neg | Negative |
| pl | Plural |
| Pos | Positive |

| | |
|---|---|
| Pst | Past |
| NonPst | Nonpast |
| RelPst | Relative past |
| RelNonPst | Relative nonpast |
| Rep | Repetitive |
| SCM | Subject concord marker |
| SIL | Société Internationale de Linguistique |
| sg | Singular |
| SVS | Simple verb stem |
| ts | topic sentence |
| V | Vowel |
| Vs | Verb stem |
| 2sg | Second person singular |
| 2pl | Second person plural |
| # | Indicates deletion or absence of an inherent element |
| * | Indicates that a form is impossible or unknown |

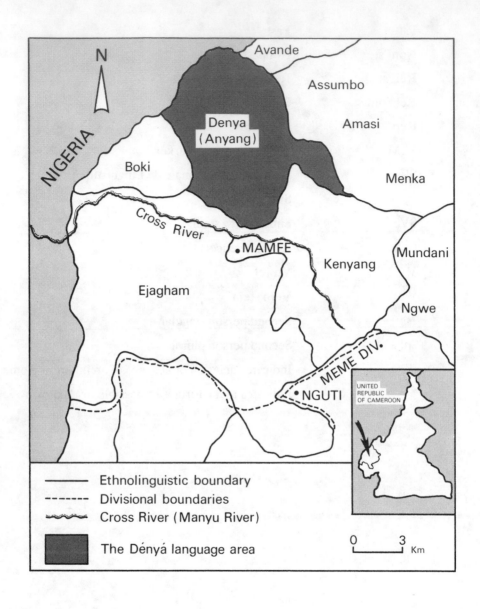

Map of Western Cameroon

# 1 Preliminary Considerations

## 1.1 The Dényá Language and People

Dényá is the native speakers' name for the language commonly referred to as Anyang (Mansfeld 1908:278; Westermann and Bryan 1970:114; Crabb 1965:11; Williamson 1971:278). Dényá is spoken by a speech community of approximately ten thousand people, according to the April 1976 publication of the General Population and Housing Census, "How Many are We?" They live in the forest areas of the Akwaya Subdivision and in some parts of Mamfe Central Subdivision in Manyu Prefecture in the Southwest Province of the United Republic of Cameroon. The majority of the speakers spread from the immediate banks of the Manyu River (Cross River) in Mamfe town westward to the border with Nigeria (see map).

Neighboring languages include Kenyang and Ejagham to the southeast and southwest respectively, Boki to the west, and Assumbo, Amasi, and Menka to the north. Distinct dialect differences exist, corresponding to such clans as Takamanda, Bitieku, Basho, and Kendem. Fr. Bruen's term for Dényá is Takamanda (cited in *Linguistic Survey of the Northern Bantu Borderland* 1956:40). The term Takamanda refers to a clan name rather than to the language as a whole. In the same source (p. 39) there is a suggestion that Anyang includes the area where Takamanda, Menka, and Assumbo are spoken. The present study is based on the dialect spoken in Assam (Takamanda) Customary Court area. It is the dialect the author speaks.

In recent studies by Tyhurst (1983), Kendem is not considered a dialect of Dényá:

> ...because of the significant differences in morphological forms that we found in the survey (e.g., noun prefixes and the verb prefix marking infinitives; (1983:40)

Tyhurst and Tyhurst (1983) recognize four dialects: Takamanda, Basho, Bitieku, and Bajwa. About Basho and Bajwa they write:

1

People from the south (Takamanda and Bitieku dialects) usually group the two northern dialects (Basho and Bajwa) as one, and they refer to it either as Basho or Bajwa. (1983:9)

With my several Kendem friends we talk to each other, each in his own dialect, without too much loss of information. That is why I continue to include Kendem as one of the Dényá dialects.

The speakers of Dényá call themselves the Anyá or Bɔ́ɔ̀: Ányá 'the Anya people'. They occupy approximately fifty villages and are, in the main, peasant farmers, hunters, and fishermen. Contending with the vast, still virgin equatorial forest, which is traversed by numerous large rivers, the Anyá eke out a living from the forests and the rivers.

The area has remained cut off from the rest of the country because of the complete absence of roads. For the same reason, though most of the Anyá are within the Akwaya Subdivision, very few have any contact with the subdivisional headquarters in Akwaya, scores of kilometers away from the nearest Anyá village. Mamfe town has remained the main center for trade, medical services, and administration.

It may be noted also that the Anyá have long had trading contacts with Nigeria, especially along the Cross River. These contacts are still maintained.

In this study whenever reference is made to earlier sources, the term Anyang is maintained. Otherwise the language is called Dényá. From the early sources there appears to have been some uncertainty as to whether or not Dényá is a Bantu language. This was due primarily to a lack of any serious linguistic investigation. Also, Anyang definitely falls outside the Bakundu-Balundu language group that comprises part of the borderline of the northwest Bantu as established by Guthrie (1967:20 ff.). Such languages were not given full status as Bantu, but were known as Semi-Bantu (Johnston 1919), Sub-Bantu (Guthrie 1967), or Bantoid.[1] Talbot (1926), cited by Westermann (1952:114), considered Anyang to be "a subsection of Banyangi." (Banyangi refers to Kenyang, which is referred to as Nyang by the Linguistic Survey [1956:39].) But Westermann stated that the speech of Anyang "appears to belong to the Ekoid Cluster." Greenberg's (1963) classification of African languages fails to mention Anyang. However, he mentions unclassified languages of Cross River, three in the Benue-Congo subfamily of the Niger-Congo language family; Anyang must have been one of those.

---

1 The investigators of the Linguistic Survey of the Northern Bantu Borderland (1956:14) applied the term Bantoid to languages in which Guthrie's second criterion of a Bantu language, "a vocabulary part of which can be related by fixed rules to a set of hypothetical common roots," does not hold good. Also, these languages have an elaborate system of class prefixes and agreements showing no regular relationship to the Bantu classes.

In an earlier investigation which led to the publication of volume one of *Linguistic Survey of the Northern Bantu Borderland* (1956), Anyang was referred to as Takamanda, but was not investigated. With reference to Takamanda and three other neighboring languages (Manka, Assumbo, and Amasi in section B among the Bantoid languages) the investigators wrote:

> During the survey they were not investigated owing to the non-availability of informants within a reasonable radius of our main points of operation. No second-hand information on these languages was obtained in the field, but as they are surrounded by Bantoid languages, e.g., the *ŊKƆM* group, *KEAQƏ NYAŊG*, and have *TIV* to the northwest, it is not improbable that they may have some of the characteristics already observed in their neighbors. (1956:40)

Recently, Crabb (1965:14–15), following Guthrie's suggestion that the Bantu borderline extended beyond the traditional northwest limit, made a more decisive statement, even though his statement might be based on fragmentary evidence. The Ekoid languages as a whole, he claimed, are Bantu languages because they have a high degree of common vocabulary among them and share some common Bantu innovations in the noun class prefixes. Williamson (1971:266) notes that Crabb uses a cover term, *Mamfe Bantu*, for a number of unclassified languages spoken around Mamfe town, one of which is Anyang. She remarks that Crabb does not consider Anyang and Kenyang to belong to the grassland group of these languages. In Crabb's view, Anyang is a Bantu language, an opinion which the author also holds.

The first linguistic data of Anyang is Mansfeld's (1908:278–305). It appears as part of a comparative word list of six languages.

## 1.2. The Present Study

For a long time linguistic description has treated the sentence as the highest grammatical unit; grammatical rules were considered to be operative within the sentence and not beyond it. Chomsky in *Syntactic Structures* (1957) reemphasized the importance of the sentence as the central unit of grammatical description.

Although it is usually accepted that a context influences a sentence (Lyons 1977:625ff.; Halliday and Hasan 1976:326–27), it is not widely held that units above a sentence should be considered as grammatical. However, some linguists, such as Longacre, Grimes, Callow, and Pike, believe that context determines the selection of sentence elements in a nonarbitrary manner. In their linguistic descriptions, they have been able to demonstrate that low-level grammatical units can be interpreted and explained within discourse.

Discourse refers to text, written or oral and of whatever length. Studies in discourse analysis have revealed that each text has its own internal structure. This point is particularly emphasized by Binam Bikoi and Soundjock (1977:6) in the following words:

La division ou structuration du texte n'est pas une pure fantaisie du critique en maille de logique: C'est de lui-même et presque de manière
autonome et interne que le texte s'organise, se planifie et se structure et
ce, par des signes linguistiques placés aux ligatures ou points stratégi-
ques du texte.

In other words, there is in every discourse a natural outline that limits and
regulates the outline the analyst may want to impose on it. It is the role of the
text analyst to be sensitive to these linguistic devices ("des signes
linguistiques") that determine the structure of its parts. Harris (1963:7), to
whom we owe the term *discourse analysis,* emphasizes the idea of a "global
structure characterizing the whole discourse."

The intent of this study, which is concerned with the use of Dényá verbs, is
to account for the function of lower-level grammatical units, namely, verb
forms, in the context of Dényá discourse structure. Verb forms in many languages involve inflectional categories such as tense, aspect, and mood which
Grimes (1975:230–37) refers to as modality elements. But Dényá is not a
highly inflectional language, and the various verb forms are all related to the
category of mood.

The term *mode* is used as a cover term for the various verb forms one may
encounter in Dényá. It is demonstrated that the relatively small number of
modes can realize a large number of discourse functions (Coulthard
1977:14) and that the type of information given depends upon the particular
discourse structure. It is also shown that a given discourse genre is characterized by a given mode. (Longacre [1976:197–201] posits four deep-structure monologue genres: narrative, procedural, expository, and hortatory.
These terms are explained later in this section.)

This study is based on data from two sources, namely, myself as a native
speaker of Dényá with intuition (in Chomsky's sense of the word) as to the
grammaticality of Dényá sentences, and from other mother-tongue speakers.
They include six men, whose ages range from fifteen to sixty, and two women.
The women are my mother and another woman, both about age fifty-five.
Two of the men live in Victoria, while the rest, including the women, live in
either Kesham or Bache villages in Akwaya Subdivision.

The corpus consists of thirty-five tape-recorded oral texts: fifteen narrative, eight procedural, six hortatory, and six expository. They were collected
between November 22 and December 31, 1979. The thirty-five texts represent some fifteen hours of recorded, freely spoken language.

The narrative texts comprise ten fictional, three personal, and two historical narratives. These texts are responses to either a question or a request to
tell a story. The personal narrative texts are responses to questions such as
"What happened yesterday/last night?" or "What did you do/kill today/last

night?" The fictional narratives were usually responses to the request, "Tell us a story."

The procedural texts consist of six prescriptive (how-to-do-it) texts and two descriptive (how-it-was-done) texts. Of the prescriptive texts, six are second-person, one is first-person, and one is third-person. These texts were collected as responses to How-questions. For example, the text on the weaving of a sleeping mat by my mother was a response to the question, "How is a sleeping mat woven?"

The expository texts were given as responses to questions such as "What is X?" or "Why is X in that state?" The length of each text and the eloquence of the speaker depended on his perception of unstated related questions.

A hortatory text is usually a response to extralinguistic conditions. For example, the departure of a son to a foreign country or a daughter to her new home after marriage may necessitate a hortatory text on the part of a parent. Most of the hortatory texts used in this study were not given in actual situations. Rather, the speakers were asked to imagine a certain situation and give an appropriate text.

After being taped, the thirty-five texts were transcribed, charted, and analyzed. The first twenty-six texts were labeled A through Z, and the remaining fourteen were labeled Aa, Bb, Cc, and so on. Only texts A-E are included here (see appendix B), although examples from some of the other texts are cited in a few places.

Where illustrative material from texts A-E is given, it bears two numbers. The first is the consecutive number used for all examples; the second refers to the sentence number in the text from which it is taken.

The texts are presented in Dényá with a morpheme-by-morpheme interlinear translation into English. Each sentence is numbered 1, 2, 3, 4, etc., and further divided into clauses 1a, 1b, 1c, etc., each of which is placed on a different line. Under each verb is its literal translation followed by an abbreviation in parentheses. This abbreviation indicates the type of mode. A free translation is given at the end of the text.

In my analysis of Dényá discourse, much help has been received from Grimes 1975, especially his distinction between events and nonevents in narrative discourse, and also from Longacre 1974 and 1976 in his distinction of four monologue genres.

Grimes describes the material in a narrative discourse as on or off the event-line. The event-line includes actions that occur in sequence or simultaneously. These events advance the story. Levinsohn (1976) refers to the event-line as *progression* and to nonevents as *digression*.

It is now recognized, by Longacre in particular, that the events in a narrative are not all of the same importance. An important event may be high-lighted, while routine and predictable ones are usually not highlighted. In this study, important events are called climactic events.

It has been possible to extend the idea of events and nonevents to other discourse types. Thus, in a procedural text, for example, the material can be either on the procedure-line or off it.

In Dényá the distinction between events and nonevents is particularly important because the use of mode in events and nonevents is different.

Grimes distinguishes four types of nonevents: setting, background, evaluation, and collateral material. These are now discussed for Dényá.

In a narrative discourse, the events occur at a certain place and time. The setting indicates when and under what conditions the events take place. There are two types of setting in a story: temporal and spatial. In Dényá narrative discourse, temporal settings are not indicated precisely but in such terms as "one day", "the next day", "in the morning", and so on. The two main spatial settings, as exemplified in text A (see appendix B), are the village and the stream. (Details about this are given in chap. 3.) Another part of the setting is the introduction of some of the main participants as part of the cast. This is more fully explained in section 3.1.1.2.

The background in a narrative is explanation and comment about what happens. Such information ensures that the audience will follow the monologue and get the point. Background material forms neither the event-line nor the setting proper, though the setting is also background. Text B in appendix B has some good examples of background. The story is about Ŋkpɛé, who, after getting married, gives laws to his wife. The purpose of the laws is to hide Ŋkpɛé's red buttocks from his wife. An example of an explanation is B 14 (a) to (f). It explains the purpose of the laws, information without which an audience would be in doubt.

Most of the fictional stories contain explanations at the conclusion. Such explanations make the story's purpose clear, though they may not be the "real" explanation — the narrator often has unstated intentions in telling the story. In text A, the narrator explains why an elephant always dies near a stream.

*Evaluation* indicates the feeling of the speaker towards some of the information. The speaker indirectly wants to influence the opinion of the audience. A good example of evaluation is seen in text H (not included in the appendix) which tells the story of *Atátá Monga*, farmer-sorcerer, whose disobedient wife dug up a yam he had asked her not to touch. The narrator expresses his feelings openly by generalizing that women are always disobedient.

*Collateral material* includes what did not happen and what might have happened. By stating what did not happen, the narrator highlights what happened. Collateral material is not common discourse information in Dényá.

As indicated, this study is not limited to narrative discourse. It extends to other discourse types as suggested by Longacre (1976:197–206; also in Longacre and Levinsohn 1978:104–22). It is his 1976 classification of discourse types that provides the basis for the rest of this study. The four deep-structure discourse genres Longacre posits are (1) narrative, (2) procedural, (3) hortatory, and (4) expository.

Narrative discourse recounts some sort of story. The events are told either in the first or third person, and they are usually in chronological sequence. Also, the events are considered to have been accomplished. Narrative discourse is used to inform or entertain.

Procedural discourse tells how something is done. It may be given in first, second, or third person. Unlike narrative discourse, which is given in accomplished time, procedural discourse is in projected time. Descriptive procedural discourse, however, is in accomplished time.

Hortatory discourse indicates correct behavior in regard to a certain situation. Its purpose is to influence or change the conduct of the addressee. It is addressee oriented. In this discourse type, time is nonfocal.

Expository discourse expounds or explains a given subject matter. It is subject-matter oriented. As in hortatory discourse, time is nonfocal.

In discussing discourse genres, Longacre states, and rightly so, that it is necessary to make a distinction between intent and form. Intent relates to deep structure, and form to surface structure. In the preceding definitions of the various genres, it is the intent that has been given: narrative to entertain or inform, procedural to tell how to do something, expository to explain or describe, and hortatory to influence conduct.

Ideally, the surface structure, which is the text, exists to encode the deep structure (intent). But, quite often there is no one-to-one relationship between the two, so the surface structure may encode something different from its primary intent. In this connection, therefore, it is not surprising to find that narrative is used to show a procedure, or to explain a subject, or even to give a lesson in morals. In such a case, the deep structure procedure, exposition, or exhortation is expressed in surface-structure narrative. The real intent may come out at certain points, however, such as when the "moral of a story" is stated at the very end.

Longacre (Longacre and Levinsohn 1978:103–4) subdivides these four major genres into sixteen different types, as represented in figure 1.

|  | + AGENT | | −AGENT | |
|---|---|---|---|---|
|  | + Tension | −Tension | + Tension | −Tension |
| + Proj T | prophecy | | how to do it | |
|  | plot/climax | episodic | | |
|  |  |  | obstacles | no obstacles |
| + Chron | — **narrative** — | | — **procedural** — | |
|  | story | | how it was done | |
|  | plot/climax | episodic | | |
| −Proj T |  |  |  |  |
|  |  |  | obstacles | no obstacles |
| + Proj T | hortatory | | future things | |
|  | argument | no argument | argument | no argument |
| −Chron | — **behavioral** — | | — **expository** — | |
|  | eulogy/speech | | current/past things | |
| −Proj T |  |  |  |  |
|  | argument | no argument | argument | no argument |

Fig. 1. Discourse genres and types

Figure 1 shows that the four discourse genres, namely, narrative, procedural, behavioral, and expository, can be divided into sixteen types. There are two primary parameters: ± chronological linkage (CHRON) and ± agent orientation. In addition, there are two other features which form secondary parameters: ± projected time (PROJ T) and ± tension.

The four main genres result from the intersection of the two main parameters. Figure 2 gives another representation of the same information.

| Genre | Agent Orientation | Chronological Linkage |
|---|---|---|
| Narrative | + | + |
| Procedural | − | + |
| Behavioral | + | − |
| Expository | − | − |

Fig. 2. The four discourse genres

Narrative is plus agent orientation, plus chronological linkage. Procedural discourse is minus agent orientation, plus chronological linkage. Behavioral discourse is similar to narrative in that it is plus agent orientation, but it is minus chronological linkage. Expository discourse is minus agent orientation and minus chronological linkage.

When the two secondary parameters are added, as in figure 1, a number of subtypes are established. When projected time is added, narrative genre divides into ordinary stories and prophecies. Prophecies are plus-projected time, and ordinary stories are minus-projected time. In this study, only ordinary stories are considered.

The same parameter applied to the procedural genre divides that kind of text into how-to-do-it and how-it-was-done. The former is plus-projected time, while the latter is minus-projected time.

Projected time divides behavioral texts into hortatory and eulogistic, and expository texts into future topics and current/past topics. These latter two are, respectively, plus-projected time and minus-projected time.

The last parameter shown in figure 1 is minus tension. A narrative text that does not contain tension or struggle is episodic. However, a lot of stories contain some tension — such stories contain plots or build up to climaxes. In the procedural genre, routine procedures are minus tension, while those that involve struggle or alternative are plus tension. In expository and behavioral discourse, where argument is assumed, it is plus tension. Those that do not involve some argument are minus tension.

This study is based on the following discourse types:

(a) Narrative:  ordinary stories with a plot/climax

(b) Procedural: a mixture of how-to-do-it and how-it-was-done, most involving some form of struggle

(c) Behavioral: hortatory texts that contain some argument

(d) Expository: current and past things that involve some argument

Longacre and Levinsohn remark that a scheme like the one just presented is "essentially a scheme of deep structure. Surface structure discourse genre often involves a skewing of the deep structure intent with the surface structure form" (1978:104).

Little work has been done on Dényá prior to this study. Therefore a sketch of the phonology and the noun class system, as well as some brief notes on order typology are included in appendix A. Chapter 2 gives a description of the verb forms. This chapter is of particular importance, providing the basis for identifying verb forms and their functions in discourse. Chapters 3 through 6 deal with the use of mode in discourse. Chapter 7, the concluding chapter, summarizes the functions of mode in the various discourse genres.

# 2 The Modes

This chapter is concerned with the verb forms in Dényá. The verb is an area in the grammar of most languages in which inflectional categories exist. Generally, these categories are viewed as being organized into four sets: mood, tense, aspect, and voice.

In Dényá, not all of these categories are inflectional. The system of voice, for example, is noninflectional; it usually involves the relationship of participants to action.

Mood, as a grammatical category, is used in two senses. First, it refers to the speaker's communicative options that serve to identify the speech act in a given clause/sentence. The speaker's communicative options might be to inform, to request information, or to command. These options give what has been traditionally recognized as the indicative (declarative), interrogative, and imperative moods. In most languages, the distinctions between indicative and imperative (but not the interrogative) are grammaticalized in the form of the verb. In Dényá the indicative is morphologically unmarked for mood, while the other two are marked. Second, mood refers to the speaker's attitude toward what he is saying (Lyons 1968:307). He may express doubt, desire, or wish. He may indicate that an event is conditioned in its occurrence, and so on. Some linguists would reserve the term *modality* for this second meaning of *mood*. In this study the term "mood" is used for both meanings.

The other two categories, tense and aspect, are of particular importance. Tense, as a grammatical category, "relates the time of the action, event or state of affairs referred in the sentence to the time of utterance" (Lyons 1969:305). It may be past, present, or future. But while all languages have ways of referring to past, present, or future time, not all languages have tense. In other words, tense is not marked as a morphological feature of verbs in all languages.

Dényá does not make tense distinctions with as much specificity as certain grassland Bantu languages. Referring to tense in Kom, Chia (1976:49)

10

writes, "As a first approximation, Kom has four past tenses, the present tense, and three future tenses."

Anderson (1980:1–11) claimed for Ngyembɔɔn-Bamileke three past tenses, an unmarked present tense, and three future tenses. Similarly, Mfonyam (personal communication) claims that Bafut has four past tenses and three future ones. Examples could be multiplied.

In Dényá, it is difficult to argue convincingly for tense, although in this work tense terminology is retained. The terms used are past (Pst) and nonpast (NonPst). The past is identical with the verb stem/root, manifested as a zero suffix. The nonpast takes a suffix represented as the {-ge1} suffix, a detailed description of which is presented in this chapter.

(1) *John    a-fomé       ŋka*
    John    he-threw     money
    'John threw away money'.

(2) *John    a-fome-ge                   ŋka*
    John    he-throws (is-throwing)     money
    'John is throwing away money' or 'John habitually throws away
    money'.

In these two examples, (1) has the ∅ form and (2) has the {-ge1} form. It can be argued tentatively that ∅ and {-ge} have semantic correlation of past and nonpast. The term *nonpast* is preferred to *present* because {-ge} does not necessarily imply contemporaneity with the act of the utterance. In (2), the action may actually be taking place at the moment of speech, or it may be habitual and therefore include the present, the past, and the future. Because of this inherent ambiguity, it is convenient to talk of it as nonpast rather than present. On the other hand, the {-ge} form does not always refer to nonpast time, as the following examples illustrate:

(3) *John    a-pyɛ-ɛ            útɔ́      cáncá*
    John    he-work{-ge1}    work    well
    'John works well' or 'John habitually works well'.

(4) *John    a-pyɛ-ɛ            ńyá         utɔ́      cáncá*
    John    he-work{-ge1}    long-ago    work    well
    'John used to work well long ago'.

In (3), the {-ge} form is used without a time adverb and conveys the meaning of nonpast. In (4), where it is accompanied by the time adverbial *ńyá* 'long ago', the form carries a past meaning. If used with the time adverbial *nyíɛ* 'soon, a while', it refers to an action in the future:

(5) *John    a-pyɛ-ɛ            nyíɛ     utɔ́*
    John    he-work{-ge1}    fut      work
    'John will work'.

Coming back to the ∅ form in Denya, notice that it needs to be accompanied by a time adverb in order to specify an exact point in the past. Another problem with the ∅ form is that it gives nonpast meanings when it combines with certain aspectual prefixes (as illustrated in the next section). It can also be argued that the ∅ and {-ge₁} forms are not primarily tense markers at all because in normal conversation the forms convey the aspectual meanings of perfective and imperfective more than time distinctions, since adverbials are needed in any case to locate the action in time.

When one examines the use of the ∅ and {-ge} forms in discourse, it soon becomes clear that they are like the other verb forms that one would rightly call modes, for example: imperative, hortative, relative, and conditional. In this study, the term *mode* has been used as a cover term for all the verb forms in Denya discourse. There are frequent references, for example, to the past mode, the nonpast mode, the conditional mode, the relative mode, and so on.

## 2.1 The Structure of the Verb

**2.1.1 Obligatory and optional elements.** In any construction in the language there is a verbal form. The verbal form normally consists of certain obligatory and optional elements, which can be diagrammed as follows, with + indicating an obligatory element and ± an optional element:

$$+ \text{Tone} \quad \underline{\phantom{xx}} \quad \underline{\phantom{xxxx}} \quad \underline{\phantom{xxxxxx}} \quad \underline{\phantom{xxx}}$$

$$\pm S \quad \pm \text{Affix 2} \quad + \text{Verb stem (Vs)} \quad \pm \text{Affix 1}$$
$$( + \text{Stem 1} + \text{Stem 2})$$

The diagram shows that a Dényá verb consists of an obligatory verb stem with a specific tone pattern and the following elements: an obligatory subjectival concord morpheme with a particular tone pattern ( + S); optionally one of the base affixes ( ± Affix 1), which must also have a tone pattern; and optionally one of the aspect affixes ( ± Affix 2) with a characteristic tone. Instead of a single stem, a construction may contain two stems ( + Stem 1 + Stem 2).

The subject concord morpheme is an important part of the verb. Though in the second person it is absent in the imperative, it is an obligatory element for all other verb forms. The choice of a particular kind of mode affix and a tone pattern gives the mode its form.

### 2.1.2 Verb stems

**2.1.2.1 Simple verb stems.** The simple verb stem (SVS) consists of one verb root which is either monosyllabic or disyllabic and always begins with a consonant. If it is monosyllabic, it may carry either high or low tone. All disyllabic stems have low tone on the first syllable and high tone on the second. Figure 3 summarizes this.

|                     Monosyllabic Stems        |       Disyllabic Stems       |
|                           CV                  |            CVV́              |
|                           CV́                 |           C V C V́           |

Fig. 3. Simple verb stem patterns

Examples of simple verb stems are given in figure 4.

| HIGH TONE VERBS | | LOW TONE VERBS | |
|---|---|---|---|
| bέ | 'announce' | sɛ | 'receive' |
| nɔ́ | 'bite' | swa | 'sweep' |
| tó | 'shoot with a stone' | pɛ | 'look at' |
| bé | 'dance' | do | 'beat' |
| bó | 'run/escape' | kɔ | 'beg' |
| bɔ́ | 'take up' | ka | 'try' |
| wá | 'kill' | fa | 'share' |
| bá | 'marry' | be | 'place a peg' |
| kpá | 'carry' | ŋme | 'throw away' |
| nyú | 'drink' | sha | 'deny' |
| kwé | 'fall' | kwe | 'play' |

| C V C V́ Stems | | C V V́ Stems | |
|---|---|---|---|
| tané | 'go out' | feé | 'remove' |
| feré | 'remove' | ʃɛέ | 'praise' |
| fwɔré | 'taste' | waá | 'rub oil' |
| feré | 'think' | fɔ́ | 'seize' |
| kɛlé | 'look for/search' | koó | 'pass' |
| bwɔlé | 'turn' | tuú | 'gather' |
| karé | 'share/divide' | biú | 'hide' |
| selé | 'tighten' | seé | 'disappear' |
| tamé | 'greet' | wiú | 'shout' |
| bɛlé | 'sleep' | tyɛέ | 'cook' |
| wané | 'sharpen' | cyɛέ | 'give' |

Fig. 4. Examples of simple verb stems

**2.1.2.2 Complex verb stems.** A complex verb stem (CVS) consists of two roots. These are called verbs in series, serial verbs, verbal combinations, or strings of verbs. Regarding serial verbs, Bamgbose writes: "The term 'serial verbal construction' or 'serial verbs' has been applied to the combination of verbs found in many West African languages where all the verbs share a common subject in the surface structure" (1974:17). Only two verbs in the language can combine with other verbs to form a serial verb construction. (In such a combination only the first verb is inflected.) The two verbs are *cwɔ́* 'come' and *jyɛ/có* 'go'. In the *jyɛ/có* variants, *jyɛ* is used in nonimperative sentences while *có* is used only in imperatives.

In a complex verb stem, the first verb carries low tone, while the second, if monosyllabic, may have either high or low tone, depending on the tone of the verb; i.e., it carries the lexical tone. A disyllabic second root morpheme carries high tone on the first syllable and low tone on the second syllable. The following are examples of sentences containing serial constructions:

> (6) (a) *John    a-jyɛ-fóme              ŋka*
>         John    he-went-threw (∅)      money
>         'John went to throw money'.
>
>     (b) *John    a-jyɛ-ɛ-fóme            ŋka*
>         John    he-go{-ge₁}-throw      money
>         'John is going to throw money'.
>
> (7) (a) *John    a-cwɔ-gbáre             Mary*
>         John    he-came-hold (∅)       Mary
>         'John came to hold Mary'.
>
>     (b) *John    a-cwɔ-ɔ-gbáre           Mary*
>         John    he-come{-ge₁}-hold     Mary
>         'John is coming to hold Mary'.

In each pair, the first example connotes the past (perfective); and the second, the nonpast (imperfective). In the nonpast examples, it is the first verb in the series that takes the suffix. Semantically, in complex verb stems, the second verb expresses the purpose of the first.

## 2.2 The Modes

The modes in Dényá can be classified into two main categories: indicative and nonindicative, each of which is subdivided further.

**2.2.1 The indicative modes.** Indicative modes are verb forms used in simple declarative statements. Broadly speaking, the indicative modes can be subdivided into nonrelative, relative, and negative. The nonrelative comprise two nonaspectual modes, past and nonpast, and three aspectual modes, inceptive, habitual, and repetitive — all of which are built on the past (∅) form. The relative comprises past and nonpast modes.

**2.2.1.1 Nonrelative indicative modes.** *Past* (Pst) and *nonpast* (NonPst) *modes* imply tense. The formal characteristics of the past and nonpast modes are better noticed when treated together (see fig. 5). Verb stems are shown in the first column of figure 5, the past form in the second, and the nonpast in the third. The past and nonpast forms are accompanied by a third person singular subject pronoun of class 1 separated from the stem by a hyphen.

For purposes of clarity, figure 5 presents the verbs in five groups. The first three groups are examples of monosyllabic verb stems; the fourth group, of disyllabic stems; the last group, examples of complex verb stems or verbs in series.

| STEM | | PAST (Ø) | | NONPAST {-ge₁} | |
|------|------|------|------|------|------|
| *sɛ* | 'receive' | *a-sɛ* | 'he took' | *a-sɛ-le* | 'he is receiving/receives' |
| *gyá* | 'split' | *a-gyá* | 'he split' | *a-gya-le* | 'he is splitting/splits' |
| *bé* | 'dance' | *a-bé* | 'he danced' | *a-be-ne* | 'he is dancing/dances' |
| *swa* | 'sweep' | *a-swa* | 'he swept' | *a-swa-ne* | 'he is sweeping/sweeps' |
| *tó* | 'shoot' | *a-tó* | 'he shot' | *a-to-me* | 'he is shooting/shoots' |
| *tɔ́* | 'clear' | *a-tɔ́* | 'he cleared' | *a-tɔ-me* | 'he is clearing/clears' |
| *shɛ* | 'abuse' | *a-shɛ* | 'he abused' | *a-shɛ-ɛ* | 'he is abusing/abuses' |
| *nyú* | 'drink' | *a-nyú* | 'he drank' | *a-nyu-u* | 'he is drinking/drinks' |
| *bɔ́* | 'take up' | *a-bɔ́* | 'he took up' | *a-bɔ-ɔ* | 'he is taking up/takes up' |
| *tané* | 'go out' | *a-tané* | 'he went out' | *a-tane-ge* | 'he is going/goes' |
| *feré* | 'remove' | *a-feré* | 'he removed' | *a-fere-ge* | 'he is removing/removes' |
| *fwɔré* | 'taste' | *a-fwɔré* | 'he tasted' | *a-fwɔre-ge* | 'he is tasting' |
| *kɛlé* | 'search' | *a-kɛlé* | 'he searched' | *a-kɛle-ge* | 'he is searching/searches' |
| *jyɛ-nyú* | 'go to drink' | *a-jyɛn-yú* | 'he went and drank' | *a-jyɛ-ɛ-nyú* | 'he is going to drink' |
| *jyɛ-bɔ́* | 'go to take' | *a-jyɛ-bɔ́* | 'he went and took' | *a-jyɛ-ɛ-bɔ́* | 'he is going to take' |
| *cwɔ-wá* | 'come to kill' | *a-cwɔ-wá* | 'he came and killed' | *a-cwɔ-ɔ-wá* | 'he is coming to kill' |
| *cwɔ-bé* | 'come to dance' | *a-cwɔ-bé* | 'he came and danced' | *a-cwɔ-ɔ-bé* | 'he is coming to dance' |

Fig. 5. Examples of past and nonpast nonrelative indicative modes

To show the person paradigm, the verb *wá* 'kill' is given in figure 6 in the past and nonpast forms.

On formal grounds, a number of observations can be made about figures 5 and 6:

(1) The first person singular and plural and second person singular and plural pronouns of the past mode have rising tone. The pronouns of

|              | PAST (∅)      | NONPAST {-ge₁}    |
|--------------|---------------|-------------------|
| I            | ŋ̌-wá          | ŋ-wa-ne           |
| you (s.)     | ɔ̌-wá          | ɔ-wa-ne           |
| he (cl. 1/9) | a-wá          | a-wa-ne           |
| we           | dě-wá         | de-wa-ne          |
| you (pl.)    | ɛnyú-dě-wá    | ɛnyú-de-wa-ne     |
| they (cl. 2) | á-wá          | á-wa-ne           |

Fig. 6. Past and nonpast person paradigm

the nonpast mode have low tone. The subject concord markers for classes 1 and 9 carry low tone in both past and nonpast. All the other concord markers (classes 2, 3, 4, 5, 6a, 6b, 7, 8, and 10) carry high tone in both modes.

(2) The past is identical in form with the stem. High tone verbs remain high and low tone verbs remain low. The disyllabic verb stems retain high tone on the last syllable. The past has zero (∅) modification.

(3) The nonpast form has a suffix. On the basis of the type of suffix, the monosyllabic stems are subdivided into three classes: (a) those containing -le, (b) those containing -me ~ -ne variants determined by vowel quality, and (c) those containing lengthening of the vowel, represented by -V. Disyllabic verb stems invariably take an additional syllable, -ge, and it is this suffix that has been selected as the morphemic representation of the nonpast.

(4) All the syllables in the nonpast (stem + suffix) carry low tone. This means that all high tone verbs, including disyllabic verb stems with high tone on the second syllable, lose the high tone. This tone pattern in nonpast forms is noteworthy because a given stem and suffix combination with a different tone pattern results in a different verb form.

(5) The various realizations of the nonpast are represented by the morphemic symbol {-ge₁}.

It may be asked whether the various forms of {-ge₁} have constraints determining their selection. The selectional rules for these forms are not yet clear since the verbs appear to fall into classes arbitrarily. However, a few observations can be made. Figure 7 provides a useful basis for these observations.

(The vowel in the stem nucleus is shown in the first column; unfilled spaces indicate that no examples have been found.)

| VOWEL | -le | | -me ~ -ne | | -V | |
|---|---|---|---|---|---|---|
| /i/ | | | | | | |
| | ti | | | | bí | |
| | tile | | | 'wipe' | bii | 'hide' |
| /e/ | | | | | | |
| | be | | bé | | te | |
| | bele | 'peg' | bene | 'dance' | tee | 'remember' |
| | | | té | | ŋme | |
| | | | tene | 'slide on' | ŋmee | 'shoot' |
| /ɛ/ | | | | | | |
| | pɛ | | bέ | | shɛ | |
| | pele | 'look at' | bene | 'announce' | shɛɛ | 'abuse' |
| | | | kpɛ | | fyɛ | |
| | | | kpene | 'enter' | fyɛɛ | 'put in' |
| /a/ | | | | | | |
| | gyá | | bá | | ta | |
| | gyale | 'split' | bane | 'marry' | taa | 'touch' |
| | jya | | swa | | sha | |
| | jyale | 'step on' | swane | 'sweep' | shaa | 'deny' |
| /ɔ/ | | | | | | |
| | | | tɔ́ | | bɔ́ | |
| | | | tɔme | 'clear' | bɔɔ | 'takc up' |
| | | | nɔ́ | | kɔ | |
| | | | nɔme | 'bite' | kɔɔ | 'beg' |
| /o/ | | | | | | |
| | | | tó | | do | |
| | | | tome | 'shoot with a stone' | doo | 'bcat' |
| /u/ | | | | | | |
| | | | | | bú | |
| | | | | | buu | 'send away' |
| | | | | | nyú | |
| | | | | | nyuu | 'drink' |

Fig. 7. Examples of {-ge₁} suffix

The following observations are based on figure 7:

(1) Membership in the -*le* class is rather limited. It appears that the syllable nucleus of this class has the distinctive feature of [-back].

(2) In the -*me* ~ -*ne* variants, -*me* is selected by stems with /ɔ/ or /o/ as nucleus; -*ne* is selected by stems with /e/, /ɛ/, or /a/. It appears that all the stem nuclei have the feature [–closed].

(3) Membership of the -V class is large. There are no vowel restrictions.

*Aspectual modes*, relating to the grammatical category of aspect, differ from the nonaspectual in that the former are marked by a prefix while the latter are marked by a suffix. These markers always occur with the past form of the verb. The subject pronouns and subject concord marker also take the same tone as the past mode.

As stated above, in Dényá the three aspectual modes are inceptive, habitual, and repetitive:

The *inceptive mode* refers to a recently started action now in progress. The focus is on the beginning of the action, though the action is ongoing. The inceptive marker is the prefix *lé*. It does not occur with the nonpast form of the verb. Example (8a) is ungrammatical (marked *) and (8b) is grammatical:

(8) (a) *\*John a-lé-wa-ne    mpɔ*
   John he-Incep-kill(NonPst) cow


 (b) *John a-lé-wá   mpɔ*
   John he-Incep-kill(∅) cow
   'John has started killing a cow'.

The *habitual mode* refers to the spread of an action, event, or state from the past through the present to the future and characterizes the person to whom the action or state is attributed. The marker for this mode is the prefix *la-*.

(9) *John a-la-wá  menyá*
  John he-Hab-kill animal
  'John kills animals'.

In example 9, the killing of animals is characteristic of John. In other words, John is a hunter.

The *repetitive mode* indicates that an action is repeated in its occurrence. It is marked by the prefix *ma-*.

(10) *John a-ma-wá   meshu*
   John he-Rep-kill (∅) elephant
   'John killed an elephant again'.

When the repeated action has not yet taken place, but is expected or predicted, the form *mage* is used. In the case of *mage*, the nonpast marker could be considered {-*ge*} a suffix to *ma* ~ rather than to the verb.

(11) *John    a-mage-wá        meshu      geyá*
     John    he-Rep-fut-kill  elephant   tomorrow
     'John will kill an elephant again tomorrow'.

There is another form *magé-* which is used to refer to repeated hypothetical actions. As above, it could be suggested that the conditional marker -*gé* (not to be confused with {-*ge1*}; see section 2.2.2.3) is suffixed to *ma-* and not to the verb.

(12) *mbɔgé  John    a-magé-wá        meshu*
     If     John    he-Rep-Cond-kill  elephant
     'if John killed an elephant again ...'

The various aspects are summarized in figure 8.

| SUBJECT PREFIX | ASPECT | VERB STEM | TENSE |
|---|---|---|---|
| | *lé-* | simple | ∅ |
| | *la-* | | |
| *a-* | | | |
| | *ma-* | | |
| | *(mage)-* | complex | |
| | *(magé)-* | | |

Fig. 8. Aspectual mode markers

Figure 8 shows that the aspectual modes must have an obligatory subject prefix, with low tone in all but the third person plural form. In the chart, the representative example of the third person singular prefix is shown in the first column. The next column shows the position of aspect markers, which are prefixes. The third column shows the class of stem: simple (see sec. 2.1.2.1) or complex (see sec. 2.1.2.2). The fourth column indicates the position of the tense marker, which is ∅ whenever an aspect marker is present.

**2.2.1.2 Relative indicative modes.** A relative mode is a verb form that functions in relative constructions. There are two types in Dényá: the relative past (RelPst) and the relative nonpast (RelNonPst).

*The relative past mode* is characterized by:

 (a) a high-tone subject prefix as well as a SCM (Subject Concord Marker) for all classes;

(b) the suffix {-*né*} for monosyllabic verb stems;

(c) a high tone on the {-*né*} suffix;

(d) in disyllabic verb stems, ∅ modification and retention of the same tone pattern. (Because of this formal difference from the nonpast morpheme, it is given a different representation.)

(13)  *mendé       yi        á-sɛlé*
      woman       who       she-take(RelPst)
      'the woman who took'

(14)  *mendé       yi        á-cwɔ-ɔ́*
      woman       who       she-came(Rel-Pst)
      'the woman who came'

(15)  *mendé       yi        á-be-né*
      woman       who       she-dance(RelPst)
      'the woman who danced'

(16)  *mendé       yi        á-fomé*
      woman       who       she-throw(RelPst)
      'the woman who threw'

Examples 13-15 have monosyllabic stems. They respectively take -*le, -ne ~ -me,* and -V suffixes. Example 16 has a disyllabic verb stem. It has no suffix and seems to carry the stem tone.

*The relative nonpast mode* is characterized by:

(a) a high-tone subject prefix, as well as SCM for all classes;

(b) the {-*ge*} suffix for both mono- and disyllabic verb stems;

(c) a high tone on the first syllable of the stem.

Examples:

(17)  *mendé       yi        á-sɛ́-le*
      woman       who       she-takes(RelNonPst)
      'the woman who takes'

(18)  *mendé       yi        á-bé-ne*
      woman       who       she-dance(RelNonPst)
      'the woman who dances'

(19)  *mendé       yi        á-cwɔ́-ɔ*
      woman       who       she-come(RelNonPst)
      'the woman who comes'

(20) *mendé      yi       á-fóme-ge*
     woman    who    she-throw(RelNonPst)
     'the woman who throws'

**2.2.1.3  Negative indicative modes.** Though for the purpose of this study, negative indicative modes have not been treated exhaustively, some forms are here presented.

*The negative past* has rising tone on the subject pronoun and the SCM class 1 and 9, high tone on the SCM class 2, etc., low tone on the verb, and *a -wɔ́* 'negative' suffix.

(21) *ǎ-wa-wɔ́*      'he didn't kill'       *á-wa-wɔ́*      'they didn't kill'

    *ǎ-kpɛ-wɔ́*    'he didn't enter'     *á-kpɛ-wɔ́*    'they didn't enter'

    *ǎ-sɛ-wɔ́*      'he didn't receive'   *á-sɛ-wɔ́*      'they didn't receive'

    *ǎ-cwɔ-wɔ́*    'he didn't come'      *á-cwɔ-wɔ́*    'they didn't come'

    *ǎ-fomé-wɔ́*   'he didn't throw'     *á-fomé-wɔ́*   'they didn't throw'

    *ǎ-belé-wɔ́*   'he didn't keep'      *á-belé-wɔ́*   'they didn't keep'

The *negative nonpast* has rising tone on the SCM class 1 and 9, high tone on the SCM of the other classes, high tone on the verb stem, and high tone on the suffix.

(22) *ǎ-wá-né*      'he is not killing'      *á-wá-né*      'they are not killing'

    *ǎ-kpɛ́-né*    'he is not entering'    *á-kpɛ́-né*    'they are not entering'

    *ǎ-sɛ́-lé*      'he is not receiving'   *á-sɛ́-lé*      'they arc not receiving'

    *ǎ-cwɔ́-ɔ́*    'he is not coming'      *á-cwɔ́-ɔ́*    'they are not coming'

    *ǎ-fómé-gé*   'he is not throwing'    *á-fómé-gé*   'thcy arc not throwing'

    *ǎ-bélé-gé*   'he is not keeping'     *á-bélé-gé*   'they are not keeping'

The *negative relative past* has high tone on the SCM of all classes, followed by *la-* 'negative'. The verb stem carries low tone and is followed by *-wɔ́* 'negative'. This form is homophonous with the negative conditional.

(23) *á-lá-wa-wɔ́*          'he who didn't kill'

    *á-lá-kpɛ-wɔ́*        'he who didn't enter'

    *á-lá-sɛ-wɔ́*          'he who didn't receive'

    *á-lá-cwɔ-wɔ́*        'he who didn't come'

    *á-lá-fomé-wɔ́*       'he who didn't throw'

    *á-lá-belé-wɔ́*       'he who didn't keep'

The negative relative nonpast has high tone on the SCM of all classes, a *la-*'negative' prefix, and (downstepped) high tone on the verb as well as on the suffix.

(24) *á-lá-wá-né*          'he who is not killing'

    *á-lá-kpé-né*          'he who is not entering'

    *á-lá-sé-lé*          'he who is not receiving'

    *á-lá-cwɔ́-'ɔ*          'he who is not coming'

    *á-lá-fómé-gé*          'he who is not throwing'

    *á-lá-bélé-gé*          'he who is not keeping'

**2.2.2 The nonindicative modes.** Nonindicative modes can be subdivided into nonconditional and conditional. The nonconditional further subdivide into imperative and insistence imperative.

**2.2.2.1 Imperative modes.** Imperative modes are divided primarily into positive and negative. The positive imperative modes are further subdivided into those that require orders to be carried out immediately and those in which the orders may be carried out at any time. These two types are referred to as "immediate" and "anytime" imperatives. A further distinction between singular and plural can be observed within the immediate imperatives. Under imperatives are classed both the second person forms that are marked by absence of SCM and the other persons that contain an obligatory SCM.

Paradigm of immediate imperative:

(25) *ŋ́-wá*          'I-(should)-kill'

    *wá*          '(you) kill'

    *á-wá*          'he-(should)-kill'

    *dé-wá*          'we-(should)-kill' or 'let us kill'

    *wá-ge*          '(you pl) kill!'

    *á-wá*          'they-(should)-kill'

Paradigm of "anytime" imperative:

(26) *ŋ́-wá-né*          'I-(should)-be-killing'

    *wá-né*          '(you) Be-killing!'

    *á-wá-né*          'he-(should)-be-killing'

    *dé-wá-né*          'we-(should)-be-killing'

    *ɛnyú-dé-wá-né*          '(you pl.) Be-killing!'

    *á-wá-né*          'they-(should)-be-killing'

The SCM carries a high tone: it is ∅ for second person singular and plural in the immediate imperative paradigm, and for second person singular in the "anytime" imperative. The verb always carries a high tone (on all the syllables) except for the second person singular immediate forms, which carry lexical tone when they are monosyllabic, but high tone when disyllabic. The second person plural forms also are special.

Compare:

(27) (a) *sɛ*    'Receive!'        *sé-ge*        '(you pl.)Receive!'

   (b) *gyá*    'Split!'          *gyá-ge*        '(you pl.) Split!'

   (c) *fómé*  'Throw!'         *fóme-ge*       '(you pl.) Throw!'

All the "anytime" forms carry high tone all the way through, just like all the nonsecond person forms.

The immediate imperative, which has a suffix in the second person plural only, is therefore similar to the past indicative form. The "anytime" imperative, on the other hand, contains a {-gé₂} suffix, which is similar to the nonpast suffix, but not identical. Compare the following examples:

(28) (a) *sé-lé*      'Receive!'  and   *a-sɛ-lɛ*      'he receives'

   (b) *kpé-né*     'Enter!'    and   *a-kpɛ-ne*     'he enters'

   (c) *cwɔ́-gé*    'Come!'     and   *a-cwɔ-ɔ*      'he comes'

   (d) *fómé-gé*   'Throw!'    and   *a-fome-ge*    'he throws'

As for the negative imperative, the verb stem is preceded by a high tone subject pronoun and is followed by a high tone suffix, *-gé* (invariant in form, not to be confused with {-ge₁} or {-gé₂}). In high-tone monosyllabic verbs, the high tone is replaced by a low tone. In disyllabic verbs, the high tone on the second syllable is maintained as in the following paradigm:

(29) *ń-wa-gé*         'I-(should)-kill-not'

   *ɔ́-wa-gé*          'you-(should)-kill-not' or 'Don't kill!'

   *á-wa-gé*          'he-(should)-kill-not'

   *dé-wa-gé*         'we-(should)-kill-not' or 'Let's not kill!'

   *ɛnyú-dé-wa-gé*    'you-(pl.)-(should)-kill-not'

   *á-wa-gé*          'they-(should)-kill-not'

**2.2.2.2 Insistence imperative modes.** There is a special insistence form for the imperative. It consists of a verb in any mode followed by the insistence form, and differs from the imperative, second person singular and plural, in that the SCM is never ∅ and the verb form is regular.

(30) (a) *ň-ké    ɔ́-wá*
         I-say   you-kill
         'I say you must kill'.

    (b) *ň-ké    ɔ́-wá-né*
         I-say   you-must-kill
         'I say you must be killing'. (See also Text E, 7b and 12c.)

**2.2.2.3 The conditional mode.** The conditional mode indicates that an action is conditioned. It is marked by the suffix *-gé* which is identical with the final syllable of the conditional marker *mbɔgé* 'if' and with that of the negative imperative. However, unlike the negative, which has high tone on the SCM, the conditional mode has low tone on the subject pronoun and the SCM classes 1 and 9, but high tone on the SCM of the other classes. The first syllable of verb stems carries low tone in the conditional mode.

(31) *mbɔgé    ɔ-sɛ-gé              mpɔ*
      if        you-receive-(cond)  cow
      'if you received a cow'

(32) *mbɔgé    ɔ-wa-gé             mpɔ*
      if        you-kill-(cond)     cow
      'if you killed a cow'

(33) *mbɔgé    ɔ-fomé-gé           ŋka*
      if        you-throw-(cond)    money
      'if you threw money'

## 2.3 Summary

The modes described in section 2 are here summarized, first, in paradigm form (restricted to the third person subject of class 1) and, second, in a tree diagram, which allows for the relationships between the modes to be observed.

**2.3.1 The verb paradigms.** In figures 10 and 11, six verbs are used to present the modes in paradigm form. Each column is headed by a number and an affix. The tone pattern for the particular mode is also indicated. Only high tone is marked. An accent mark over SCM means that the SCM of class 1 carries the high tone. Tone, whether high or low, is also marked over V to show the tone carried by the verb stem. Absence of a tone mark indicates lexical tone; Ø indicates absence of a tense marker. For the sake of completeness, the two imperative forms have been separated from the others.

From these paradigms it becomes clear that the modes in Dényá are marked by relatively few affixes. The importance of tone in distinguishing verb forms can also be seen.

The numbering in figures 10 and 11 is explained in figure 9.

| NO. | Affix | Tone Pattern | M O D E |
|---|---|---|---|
| 1 (a) | SCM - | V - ∅ | past |
| 1 (b) | SCM - | *lé* - V - ∅ | inceptive |
| (c) | SCM - | *la* - V – ∅ | habitual |
| (d) | SCM - | *ma* - V - ∅ | repetitive |
| 2 | SCM - | V̀- {*ge₁*} | nonpast |
| 3 | SĆM - | V̀- {*né*} | relative past |
| 4 | SĆM - | V́ - {*ge₁*} | relative nonpast |
| 5 | SCM - | V̀- *gé* | conditional |
| 6 (a) | ∅ - | V - ∅ | 2s imperative (immediate) |
| (b) | ∅ - | V - *ge* | 2p imperative (immediate) |
| (c) | ∅ - | V - {*gé₂*} | 2s imperative (anytime) |
| 7 (a) | SĆM - | V -∅ | imperative (immediate) |
| (b) | SĆM - | V - {*gé₂*} | imperative (anytime) |
| 8 | SĆM - | V̀- *gé* | negative imperative |

Fig. 9. Verb modes

**2.3.2 The relationships between the modes.** Although throughout the discussion in section 2 emphasis has been on the formal characteristics of the modes, it has also been shown that the modes are related. The tree diagram in figure 12 represents these relationships.

As shown in figure 12, Dényá modes can be subdivided into two categories: indicative and nonindicative. Within the indicative, there is further subdivision into relative and nonrelative. Within the relative, there is a distinction between relative past and relative nonpast. In the nonrelative, modes subcategorize into aspectual and nonaspectual. Of the aspectual, there are three types: inceptive, habitual, and repetitive, and of the nonaspectual, there are two subgroups: past and nonpast.

Nonindicative modes divide into conditional and nonconditional. The nonconditional forms fall into two main subgroups: imperatives (second person) and insistence imperatives (nonsecond person, i.e., "other person"). The imperatives are subdivided into positive and negative, and positive imperatives are further subdivided into immediate and "anytime" imperatives. Within the immediate imperatives there is a singular form and a plural. Insistence imperatives also are subdivided into positive and negative, and the positive are subdivided into immediate and anytime. The negative imperative has the same form in all persons. (The numbers in parentheses at the bottom of the tree diagram in fig. 12 refer to the numbers in fig. 9.)

| STEMS | | 1(a)<br>SCM-V – ∅ | 1(b)<br>SCM-lé-V∅ | 1(c)<br>SCM-la-V – ∅ | 1(d)<br>SCM-ma-V – ∅ |
|---|---|---|---|---|---|
| wá | 'kill' | a-wá | a-lé-wá | a-la-wá | a-ma-wá |
| kpɛ | 'enter' | a-kpɛ | a-lé-kpê | a-la-kpê | a-ma-kpê |
| sɛ | 'receive' | a-sɛ | a-lé-sê | a-la-sê | a-ma-sê |
| cwɔ́ | 'come' | a-cwɔ́ | a-lé-cwɔ́ | a-la-cwɔ́ | a-ma-cwɔ́ |
| fomé | 'throw' | a-fomé | a-lé-fóme | a-la-fóme | a-ma-fóme |
| belé | 'keep' | a-belé | a-lé-béle | a-la-béle | a-ma-béle |

| STEMS | | 2<br>SCM-V̀{-ge₁} | 3<br>SĆM-V̀{-né} | 4<br>SCM-V̀{-gè₁} |
|---|---|---|---|---|
| wá | 'kill' | a-wa-ne | á-wa-né | á-wá-ne |
| kpɛ | 'enter' | a-kpɛ-ne | á-kpɛ-né | á-kpé-ne |
| sɛ | 'receive' | a-sɛ-le | á-sɛ-lé | á-sé-le |
| cwɔ́ | 'come' | a-cwɔ-ɔ | á-cwɔ-ɔ́ | á-cwɔ́-ɔ |
| fomé | 'throw' | a-fome-ge | á-fo-mé | á-fóme-ge |
| belé | 'keep' | a-bele-ge | á-be-lé | á-béle-ge |

Fig. 10. Paradigms of indicative modes.

| STEMS | | 5<br>SCM-V̀-gé | 6(a)<br>∅-V-∅ | 6(b)<br>∅-Vgè | 6(c)<br>∅-V{gè₂} |
|---|---|---|---|---|---|
| wá | 'kill' | a-wa-gé | wá | wá-ge | wá-né |
| kpɛ | 'enter' | a-kpɛ-gé | kpɛ | kpé-ge | kpé-né |
| sɛ | 'receive' | a-sɛ-gé | sɛ | sé-ge | sé-lé |
| cwɔ́ | 'come' | a-cwɔ-gé | cwɔ́ | cwɔ́-ge | cwɔ́-gé |
| fomé | 'throw' | a-fomé-gé | fómé | fóme-ge | fómé-gé |
| belé | 'keep' | a-belé-gé | bélé | béle-ge | bélé-gé |

| STEMS | | 7(a)<br>SĆM-V∅ | 7(b)<br>SĆM-V{-gé₂} | 8<br>SĆM-V-gé |
|---|---|---|---|---|
| wá | 'kill' | á-wá | á-wáné | á-wa-gé |
| kpɛ | 'enter' | á-kpê | á-kpé-né | á-kpɛ-gé |
| sɛ | 'receive' | á-sɛ | á-sé-lé | á-sɛ-gé |
| cwɔ́ | 'come' | á-cwɔ́ | á-cwɔ-gé | á-cwɔ-gé |
| fomé | 'throw' | á-fómé | á-fómé-gé | á-fomé-gé |
| belé | 'keep' | á-bélé | á-bélé-gé | á-belé-gé |

Fig. 11. Paradigms of nonindicative modes

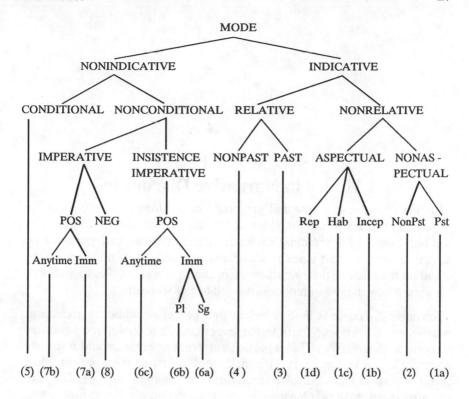

Fig. 12. A tree diagram of the modes.

# 3 Modes in Narrative Discourse

In this chapter, the internal structure of a Dényá narrative text is presented in terms of the functions of the units composing it. These units are not lower-level grammatical ones like sentences and paragraphs. Rather, a narrative text is seen as a drama or plot, and its units are established on the basis of their significance in the story as a whole. In addition, it is shown how the use of modes is related to this structure.

Narrative discourse is used to relate to a hearer or audience a chain of events such as a first- or third-person experience, a folktale, or a historical account. Such a discourse has a participant-event orientation and is usually in chronological sequence. It is normally told in first or third person. Most narrative texts in Dényá involve some form of tension or struggle. They are well structured, each part having a particular function within the plot.

## 3.1 The Internal Structure of a Narrative Text

There are three clearly discernible major parts in any Dényá narrative text: (1) introduction, (2) body, and (3) conclusion. Each of these parts is further subdivided, as the following analysis shows.

**3.1.1 Introduction.** The introduction consists of two main components: the speaker-hearer relationship and the stage.

**3.1.1.1 Speaker-hearer relationship.** A relationship with his audience is established by a narrator at the beginning of a story. The narrator does not just plunge into his narration of the events. He needs some "preparation" before beginning his actual narration. First he must link himself with the audience. This relationship is usually maintained throughout the story and in a number of ways. In fictional narratives the following devices are used to involve the audience:

**Cry and response:** In a Dényá fictional narrative, the discourse opens with a formulaic expression *ɛkame yɔɔ*, and a formulaic verbal response is expected from the audience, *yɔɔ*. *Ɛkame* means 'story', but *yɔɔ* is untranslatable. The purpose of this expression is to alert the audience, to put them in a mood for the story, and to invite them to come and listen to the story. In very long stories, the speaker may from time to time repeat this expression if, for example, he notices that the audience is falling asleep, especially the younger ones. "Cry and response" also usually announces the end of the story, calling on each one to draw his own conclusions.

Another formulaic expression, a translatable one, which follows ɛkame yɔɔ, is gé-ó. This expression consists of the imperative form of the verb "see" plus the sentence-final particle ó, indicating an invitation to do something. In this case, it is an invitation to listen and learn how certain events occurred. No verbal response is expected from the audience. Gé-ó serves as link between the ceremonial opening and the real introduction of the story.

Instead of saying gé-ó, the narrator may inform the audience of his intention to tell a particular story. He usually refers to himself in the first person and gives a preview of the story as in the following example (from text K which is not included in appendix B):

(34) Nar:    ɛkame    yɔɔ
             story     [call for response]
     Aud:    yɔɔ
             [response]
     Nar: (a) n-cwɔ-ɔ    gáre         genó
             I-come      tell(NonPst)  thing

         (b) yigé     gé-pyé-gé
             which    it-made (Rel-Pst)

         (c) ne      mekwɛnde    á-la-á
             and     pig         he-who remained(RelPst)

             mbɔ        mbaá    mango    ne      meno
             like-that  place   to-dig   with    mouth

Free translation:

> [Nar:] 'Listen to a story'. [Aud:] 'We listen'. [Nar:] 'I am going to tell you what made Pig remain a digger of the earth with his mouth'.

What this example illustrates is that the speaker-hearer relationship may include the theme, or topic, of the story. However, not all texts have the theme thus stated — texts A and B in appendix B, for example.

**Songs:** The speaker-hearer relationship in parts of the story other than the introduction may take the form of songs, repetitions, digressions, rhetorical questions, evaluations, etc. Only songs found in a number of texts used for this study are illustrated here.

One such text tells the story of *Atátá Moŋga*, a farmer-sorcerer whose disobedient wife dug up a yam he had forbidden her to dig. In the story, *Atátá Moŋga* went to a land of the spirits. In his absence, his wife and six of his children, the crippled one excepted, ate the forbidden yam and died. Nobody knew how to go find *Atátá Moŋga*, in order to inform him of what had happened. Peacock finally volunteered to go. The following song is Peacock's message to *Atátá Moŋga*.

(35) Nar: *kwére kɔkɔ, kwére kwére kɔkɔ kwére kɔkɔ, Atátá Moŋga*

       Aud: *kwére kɔkɔ, kwére kwére kɔkɔ, kwére kɔkɔ*

       Nar: *Atátá Moŋga*

       Aud: *kwére kɔkɔ kwére kwére kɔkɔ, kwére kɔkɔ*

       Nar: *genyɛ*     *yígé*     *ɔ́-jɔɔ́*     *mbɔ*
           yam       which    you-said   like-that

       Aud: *kwére kɔkɔ, kwére kwére kɔkɔ, kwére kɔkɔ*

       Nar: *ɔ-ké*       *muú*     *aá-cogé*
           you-said   person   he-dig-not

       Aud: *kwére kɔkɔ, kwére kwére kɔkɔ, kwére kɔkɔ*

       Nar: *mendé*    *wiɛ*    *a-jyɛ*     *có*
           wife       your    he-went   dug

       Aud: *kwére kɔkɔ, kwére kwére kɔkɔ, kwére kɔkɔ*

       Nar: *a-nyɛ́*     *mɛtɛ*    *a-gbó*
           she-ate    already   she-died

       Aud: *kwére kɔkɔ, kwére kwére kɔkɔ, kwére kɔkɔ*

       Nar: *baá*      *bíɛ*    *á-gbó*    *ako*
           children   your   they-died   all

       Aud: *kwére kɔkɔ, kwére kwére kɔkɔ, kwére kɔkɔ.*

The song consists of leading lines sung by the narrator followed by an onomatopoeic refrain by the audience, suggesting the sound made by the peacock. The leading lines contain part of the message. The function of this song is to furnish the audience with information unknown to the other participant in the narrative. A song such as this has a teaching function because it will be remembered long after the narrative is forgotten — the consequences of disobedience are embodied in the song.

**3.1.1.2 The stage.** The stage introduces the temporal and spatial setting, as well as the cast of participants and the situation. The time setting for the speaker-hearer relationship must be kept separate from the time setting of the discourse as a whole. In the peacock text previously quoted, the time setting for the speaker-hearer relationship is the here and now, that is, the moment of speaking. It is not the time setting for the story as a whole. For a story as a whole, the narrator usually establishes a time base relative to the moment of speaking; and in personal narratives, the time base may be set at a recent past by the use of an appropriate time adverbial. In the following example the time base is *yesterday:*

(36) *ŋjuú na,     εwi έ-pyε-έ                        me*
     yesterday   the-one it-which-made(RelPst)   me

'Yesterday there was something which happened to me'.

This example could be the introductory sentence to a whole narrative of identified events that occurred yesterday.

**(1) Temporal setting.** In fictional narrative, the narrator may set the time base in the following ways:

(a) In a number of texts studied, the time base was set with time words that do not indicate a specific time in the past. They merely state that there was a certain time. An example of this is seen in text A.

(b) The temporal setting, more frequently, is established by a timeless expression, namely, a stative clause. However, the audience interprets the events as having taken place in the past. Quite often the narrator uses a stative that implies that a certain man or thing existed in the past, but no longer exists today.

(37) *gέ-ó,     Ŋkpεέ   ne    á-bɔ́     á-lú*
     see       Ŋkpεέ   and   he-was   he-is

'See, there was (but no longer is) (RelNonPst) *Ŋkpεέ*'.

(c) Once the basic time has been given, the story advances as if the events were recent until a new base is established. In such a case, more specific time words may be used. Sentences 1–20 of text B in the appendix illustrate the use of time words. Such words occur in sentence 4 (*ne ujía* 'and one morning'), sentence 6 (*újiá* 'one morning'), sentence 13 (*újiá biífɔ* 'one morning on a certain day'), sentence 15 (*ne bií bímbɔ* 'and that day'), and sentence 20 (*újiagé* 'following morning'). The introduction of a new time base usually implies the introduction of a new set of significant events. In Dényá, fictional narratives are time-oriented narratives.

**(2) Spatial setting** refers to the location where the events take place. Normally, there is a setting for the discourse when the story begins, but new settings may be established as the story progresses.

In the fictional narratives analysed for this study, the initial location is made explicit in the introduction. The main participant is often introduced in an existential clause without specifying his location. However, such narratives make numerous cultural assumptions. In the case of a main participant, the speaker makes certain assumptions about where that participant should be. Since animals are usually given human characteristics in these stories, it is assumed that a particular character must be in his home in the village. It is only when a character starts acting that he goes away from the initial setting. The following extract from text A illustrates this point:

(38) 3(b) *gebé    géfɔ́    gébɔ́    gé-lú*
            time    Indef   it       (Attr)

    (c) *ɛyígé    meshu      á-nɛ-né                        ɛpaá*
        when    Elephant   he-who-invited(RelPst)    feast

    4(a) *a-ké*
         he-said(Pst)

    (b) *á-jyé*
        they-go(ImpImm)

    (c) *á-tɔ́                       mekɔ́    wuú*
        they-clear(ImpImm)    farm     his

    5(a) *á-fé*
         they-went(Pst)

    (b) *á-tɔ́                     mekɔ́    ntó     nemeé*
        they-cleared(Pst)    farm     also    lot

    (c) *mekɔ́    ɛ-ŋéa*
        farm      it-big(Attr)

    6(a) *ne    á-tané*
         and   they-left(Pst)

    (b) *á-wilé                     muu*
        they-returned(Pst)    home

3(b) 'There was a time (c) when Elephant invited (people) to a feast.

4(a) He asked people (b) to go and (c) clear his farm.

5(a) They went (b) and did clear a big farm, (c) the farm was really big.

6(a) Then they left (the farm), and (b) returned home'.

In this extract, *meshu* is said to exist. There was nothing eventful about him yet. So he was in the village. In 5(a) to (c), *meshu* and his fellow villagers have left the village and are at the farm. In 6(a) they have left the farm to return to the village. 6(b) shows that they arrived back home. Words like *tané* 'left' and *wilé* 'returned' establish the village as the setting for the events of the story. The village remains the setting for the story until a new setting is established later.

In a narrative discourse, a new location is established when a participant leaves one location, previously established, and arrives at a new one, which then becomes the setting for a new set of actions. The following extract from text A illustrates the point:

(39) 13(a) *átá      meshu      a-tɔ́          εtε*
        Papa Elephant   he-sent(Pst)   Duiker

    (b) *ńnó      a-jyε-cwέ          manaá ne      maá nnyi*
       so-that   he-fetched(Pst)   water   from   stream

   14    *εtε      a-fé*
       Duiker   he-went(Pst)

   15(a) *a-kwɔné          maá nnyi*
       he-arrived(Pst)   stream

    (b) *a-jya          ntaá*
       he-stepped-on(Pst)   stone

  13(a) 'Papa Elephant sent (b) Duiker to go and fetch him water from the stream.

  14 Duiker went.

  15(a) He reached the stream (b) and stepped on a stone'.

In 13–14 a new location has not yet been established. In 13 it is asserted that Elephant dispatched Duiker to a stream, and in 14 it is added that Duiker actually left for that place. But it is only in 15(a) that we find a new location established with the verb *kwɔné* 'arrived'. In 15(b) a new set of actions is begun. It is important to note that in this particular text, the two locations are maintained until the end. The participants move to and from them. *εtε*, the errand boy and messenger, leaves this second location, the stream, with a message from Crab to Elephant in the village. On receiving the message, Elephant leaves immediately for the second location. In fact, he dies upon arrival there.

(3) **Cast of participants.** In addition to the time and space setting, the stage also includes the cast, that is, the characters being talked about in a narrative. All the participants in a story are the cast of participants.

A participant in Dényá narrative discourse may be a main or minor character, a villain or the victim of villainy. In the fictional narratives studied, all the participants are referred to in the third person, but usually one of them is more important than the rest.

Among third person participants, Grimes (1975:131) makes a distinction between participants and props. Participants are always animate and they normally initiate actions. Props, which may be animate or inanimate, never initiate action. Levinsohn (in Longacre and Levinsohn 1978) makes a threefold classification of participants: initiator, undergoer, and prop.

In narrative texts in Dényá, every participant must be introduced. The way a participant is introduced is indicative of his importance. A main character is first introduced with his proper name. This is illustrated by *meshu* 'Elephant' in A 3(c) and by *ŋkpɛé* in B 3(b). Occasionally, a main participant may be referred to with a generic noun rather than by name in the introductory clause; however, in the next clause he must be named, as, for example, in the following from text H (one of the texts on which this study is based, but not included in appendix B):

(40) (a) *gé-ó*
    see(Imp)

  (b) *maá    mende   áwú    ne    á-lú*
      child    man    certain  and  he-is-the-one-who(RelNonPst)

  (c) *a-kame-ge*          *Atátá  Moŋga*
      he-answers-to(NonPst)  *Atátá  Moŋga*

In 40 (b), the main character is vaguely introduced by 'there was a certain man', and in (c) he is named as *Atátá Moŋga*.

A minor character is never introduced in the introduction to a Dényá fictional narrative. When such a character does appear, he does so suddenly and without being identified; he also leaves the stage unannounced. Like main participants, minor ones may also be introduced with stative clauses anywhere in the text and renamed when they start acting.

After a participant has been introduced, whether in the introduction or later during the main events, he is repeatedly referred to as the story progresses. Normal reference to him is by either a pronoun or a demonstrative. However, very frequently, the participants are renamed.

A few rules governing participant reference in Dényá are now given. Figure 13 gives the scheme of participant reference in text A (see appendix B). The chart has four columns, which represent the ranking of the participants. Column 1 is for the main or primary participant who initiates the action. Column 2 is for the second most important participant; column 3 is for lesser participants; and column 4 is for props.

| | 1 | 2 | 3 | 4 |
|---|---|---|---|---|
| 3c | *meshu*     *a-* 'Elephant' | | | |
| 4a | *a-* | | | |
| b | | *á-* 'they' | | |
| c | *wuú* 'for him' | *á-* | | *mekɔɔ́* 'farm' |
| 5a | | *á-* | | *mekɔɔ́* |
| b | | | | |
| c | *mekɔɔ́ ɛ-* 'farm it' | | | |
| 6a | | *á-* | | |
| b | | *á-* | | |
| 7a | *meshu*    *a-* | | | *menyɛɛ́* 'food' |
| b | *a-* | | | |
| c | *a-* | | | |
| d | | *á-* | | *menyɛɛ́* |
| 8 | | *á-* | | *menyɛɛ́* |
| 9a | *a-* | | | *menyɛɛ́* |
| b | *aá-* | *negía* 'Crab' | | |
| 10 | | *negía a-* | | |
| 11a | | *negía a-* | *- ne muú* 'with person' | |
| b | | | *yi á-tyɛ́ɛge* *á-cyɛ́ɛge* 'he gives' | *menyɛɛ́* 'who he cooks' |
| c | *meshu* '(to) Elephant' | | | |
| 12a | | *a-* | | |
| b | | | *a-* 'cook' | *ŋkale dɔɔ́* 'pepper much' |
| 13 a | *átá meshu* | *a-* | *ɛtɛ* 'Duiker' | |
| b | | | *a-* 'Duiker' | *manaá* 'water' |
| 14 | | | *ɛtɛ a-* | |
| 15a | | | *a-* | |
| b | | | *a-* | |
| 16a | | *negía a-* | | |
| b | | *a-* | | |
| c | | | *ndé mú á-* 'what person he' | |
| 17a | | | *ɛtɛ a-* 'Duiker he' | |

| 1 | 2 | 3 | 4 |
|---|---|---|---|
| b | | *lé me, ɛtɛ*<br>'it's I, Duiker' | |
| c | | *ń-* I | |
| 18a | *negía a-*<br>'Crab he' | *ji* 'him' | |
| b | *a-* | | |
| c | | *ɔ́-* 'you' | |
| 19a | | *ɛtɛ a-* 'Duiker he' | |
| b | | *ň-* 'I' | *manaá* 'water' |
| c *átá meshu*<br>'Papa Elephant' | *ň-* | | |
| 20a | *negía a-* | *ne ji* 'to him' | |
| b *átá meshu yi á-* | | | *menyɛέ* 'food' |
| c *á-* 'he' | *me* 'me' | | *manaá* |
| d | | *ɔ́-* 'you' | *manaá* |
| e *ji* 'him' | | *ɔ́-* 'you' | |
| 21a | | | *manaá m ímbɔ*<br>*má-* 'water that it' |
| b *ji* | | Ø (Imp) | |
| 22a | | *ɛtɛ a-* | |
| b *meshu* | | *a-* | |
| c | | *a-* | |
| d | *negía a-* | | *manaá* |
| e | *a-* | | |
| f | | *ń-* 'I' | |
| 23a *meshu metɔ́ɔ́ é-*<br>'Elephant heart it' | | | |
| b *a-* 'he' | | | *ne gelu geŋkale*<br>'with power pepper' |
| c *ji metɔ́ɔ́*<br>'him heat' | | *yí gé-* 'which it' | |
| 24a *a-* | | | |
| b *ji a-* | | | |
| c *a-* | *negía* | | |
| d | *ɔ́-* 'you' | | |
| 25a *a-* | | | |
| b *a-* | | | |

Fig. 13. Participant reference in text A

Figure 13 shows that text A consists of main, or primary, participant *meshu* 'Elephant'. The second main participant is *negía* 'Crab', and a lesser participant is *ɛtɛ* 'Duiker'. The props in the story are *mekɔ́* 'farm', *menyɛ́* 'food,' *ŋkale* 'pepper,' and *manaá* 'water'.

The following rules apply to participant reference and reidentification in Dényá narrative discourse:

(a) When a primary participant is subject of a main verb, whether agent or not, he is subject, referred to by pronoun, of all subsequent verbs until there is another agent. After another agent has acted, the participant is reidentified, as in 3(c), 4(a), 23(a,b) in figure 13.

(b) When a second main participant is agent of a main verb, he is pronoun agent of all subsequent verbs until another agent is identified. This is illustrated by 10 and 11 in figure 13.

(c) Reference to lesser participants is governed by the same rules as is reference to second main participants.

(d) As regards reidentification, or renaming, of participants, the distinction between primary, second main, or lesser does not appear significant in Dényá. By contrast, in Guarayu of Bolivia (Newton 1978) the main character is the least named. The basic rule of thumb for renaming participants in Dényá is that the agent of a series of actions is named at the beginning of the first action. Once a participant is acting, he is in focus, and others are out of focus. When a participant comes into focus again, he has to be renamed. The main participant is always renamed at the conclusion of the story.

**3.1.2 Body.** The body, or main part, of a narrative text is composed of one or more episodes. An episode is defined here as a unit within a discourse characterized by preparatory, climactic, and postclimactic events. In a multi-episode narrative, one of the episodes is the main (climactic) one and the others are preparatory or postclimactic.

The problem (conflict) in a story and the subsequent complications are introduced in the preparatory episodes while the main episode includes the actual climax and the resolution of the conflict. In this connection, therefore, the structure of a multi-episode narrative reflects the structure of a single-episode story. This can be seen clearly, for example, in text B (see appendix B).

In text B there are two episodes. The first (6-27) deals with *Ŋkpɛɛ́'s* attempt to hide a defect from his newly married wife by giving her some laws, which she then breaks. She discovers the defect and then threatens divorce.

The second episode (29-48) shows that the wife has decided to divorce her husband, who then tries to outwit her. Then reconciliation is made.

In terms of the plot as a whole, episode 1 is preparatory to episode 2 in that all that happens in episode 1 is an attempt by the husband to prevent his wife from deciding to divorce him. She does divorce him in episode 2. It is now a real challenge to Ŋkpεέ to save the situation; in fact, this is the main part of the story. A close study of the text shows that each of the episodes falls into three sections:

Episode 1 (6-27): 1. Preparation (6-14) The problem is created when Ŋkpεέ gives his wife some laws to hide his defect, but his drunkenness exposes him. 2. Climax (15-22) The wife breaks the laws, discovers the defect, and threatens divorce. 3. Resolution (23-27) Ŋkpεέ appeases her and has temporary success. Linkage (28) Episode 2 (29-48) 1. Preparation (29-32) Divorce is decided. 2. Climax (33-47) Ŋkpεέ outwits his wife. 3. Resolution (48) Reconciliation is effected.

In Dényá an episode as a whole usually has temporal setting marked by time adverbial phrases, such as *újiá* 'in the morning the following day', *bii rama*, 'one day', and *bii fɔ́* 'a certain day'. Once the overall base for an episode has been set, events move as if they were recent until a new time base is set within the episode.

A number of linguistic devices, including role structure, stylistic devices, and verb forms, are used to signal the preparation, the climax, and the resolution. The use of verb forms is treated in section 3.2.

Role structure refers to the way the initiative passes from one participant to another, with one participant taking a more active part in a given section of the text than the others. In text B, for example, the action passes back and forth between Ŋkpεέ and his wife.

In the preparatory events of an episode, there is an aggressor who takes all the initiative. This is illustrated in the preparatory events of episode 1 of text B, where Ŋkpεέ is the one acting all the time. He gives laws (6-12), he drinks, and becomes drunk (13). His drunkenness (and then his sleep) temporarily remove him from the scene of action, so the role structure has to be changed.

Climactic events are marked by changed role structure. The victim now becomes the aggressor; thus it is Ŋkpεέ's wife who acts. She carries a light into the husband's room (15); then she threatens divorce (18-22). Now she is the aggressor and in a more powerful bargaining position than her husband.

In the resolution, the action returns to Ŋkpεέ, who attempts to appease his wife; however, he is in a much weaker position than in the preparatory events. *Ŋkpɛɛ́*, the law giver, has become the suppliant.

The second episode reveals the reverse role structure. In the preparation (29-32) the wife is acting. She decides on divorce, packs her things, leaves the home, and goes to look for another husband. The climax (33-47) shows *Ŋkpɛɛ́* taking the initiative, and he outwits her. The resolution (48) shows her acting again, but not as the aggressor. She returns to her husband, and there is reconciliation.

Grammatically, role structure is marked by the performer of each action being encoded as subject in the clauses in which he or she is mentioned. In each section the main participant is identified by his or her semantic role as actor.

The climax, or peak, in Dényá narrative discourse is signalled by several devices. Two of these devices are considered here: direct speech and concentration of participants.

(1) Direct speech. The climax is usually marked by the use of direct speech, which heightens vividness. In episode 1 of text B, for example, the climax comes when the wife discovers her husband's defect. Here the narrator shifts from reported to direct speech. Though there is no other person there, she speaks her thoughts as if she were addressing someone. She even uses rhetorical questions, for example, "So, the man I am married to has red buttocks?" dramatizing her discovery. In episode 2, the climactic events are *Ŋkpɛɛ́'s* attempt to outwit his wife, and this encounter with her is expressed mainly in direct speech.

(2) Concentration of participants. A climax can also be signalled by the concentration of participants. Usually all the main participants are involved. In episode 1, although *Ŋkpɛɛ́* is asleep and his wife is fuming with anger, his presence is significant. In text K, the tortoise, a debtor to the pig, has been deceiving the pig and uses all sorts of tricks to keep away from him. The climax is in the third episode. Here, the three main participants, namely, the tortoise, his wife, and the pig are all brought together face to face; and in this case the dialogue shifts from the pig and the tortoise's wife to the pig and the tortoise himself.

**3.1.3 Conclusion.** In the conclusion, which is the third major part of a narrative text, the speaker returns to the speaker-hearer dimension and may give an explanation, a statement of the result of the events, a moral, or the topic repeated from the introduction. A conclusion may contain one or more of these.

It has been pointed out that the formulaic expressions *ɛkame yɔɔ* and *gɛ́-ó* mark the beginning of a narrative folk tale. These expressions serve the purpose of attracting the attention of the audience. At the conclusion another formulaic expression, *gé ŋkaá wú* 'that is the reason why . . .' marks the beginning of the end. It is used to give explanations, as in the following from text B:

(41) 49(a) *gé ŋkaá wú*
          see(ImpImm) reason why

      (b) *ne á-jɔɔ-ge*
          and they-say (RelNonPst)

      (c) *mala bɔ ŋkpɛɛ ma-lu mámá*
          buttocks *Ŋkpɛɛ* they-are(NonPst) one

      (d) *ne ńtó ńnó refya re-pwɔ uto*
          and also how cunning it-more strength

      (a) 'That is why (b) it is said (c) that all *ŋkpɛɛ́* have red buttocks and (d) that cleverness is more than strength'.

In this example of a conclusion, the speaker-hearer dimension is seen in that the speaker addresses the audience and gives an explanation as well as a moral.

It should be emphasized before leaving this section that introductions and conclusions in Dényá do not form part of the event-line of the narrative.

### 3.2 The Use of Modes in Narrative Discourse

Dényá verb modes that are relevant to narrative discourse include:

1. Past (Pst)

2. Nonpast (NonPst)

3. Imperative (Imp)

4. Relative
     Relative Past (RelPst)
     Relative Nonpast (RelNonPst)

5. Aspectual
     Inceptive (Incep)
     Repetitive (Rep)
     Habitual (Hab)

At the deep-structure level only the past mode is associated with the narrative genre. The nonpast, imperative, and relative modes, it must be emphasized, are features of surface, not deep structure. The aspectual modes, which are characteristic of the deep structure of the other genres, may appear in special places in a narrative discourse.

**3.2.1 The past mode (Pst).** Generally, the past mode is used to indicate an event that was completed prior to the moment of speaking. This mode is found in the deep structure narrative genre where it is used mainly within the body of texts. Since its primary function is to advance the event-line and no story starts or ends abruptly, this mode is not found in introductions or conclusions. Within the body of a discourse, past is used with preparatory events, and it indicates that more is to be expected. Below, a long extract from text A is quoted to illustrate the point.

(42) 4(a) *a-ké*
         he-said (Pst)

   (b) *á-jyé*
         they-go(ImpImm)

   (c) *á-tó*              *mekɔɔ́*   *wuú*
         they-clear(ImpImm)   farm   his

  5(a) *á-fɛ́*
         they-went(Pst)

   (b) *á-tó*              *mekɔɔ́*   *ntó*   *nemeé*
         they-cleared(Pst)   farm   also   lot

   (c) *mekɔɔ́*   *é-ŋéa*
         farm      it-big(Attr)

  6(a) *ne*    *á-tané*
         and   they-left(Pst)

   (b) *á-wilé*           *muu*
         they-returned(Pst)   home

  7(a) *meshu*   *a-tyɛé*         *menyɛé*
         Elephant   he-prepared(Pst)   food

   (b) *a-cyɛé*
         he-gave(Pst)

   (c) *a-ké*
         he-said(Pst)

   (d) *á-nyé*
         they-eat(ImpImm)

  8   *á-nyɛ́*      *menyɛé*   *ká*   *káká*
         they-ate(Pst)   food      for   long

  9(a) *a-karé*        *menyɛé*
         he-divided(Pst)   food

(b) *ǎ-cyɛέ-fɔ́*          *negiá  wɔ́*
he-gave-really not (PstNeg)  Crab  neg

10   *negía     a-lu    mbɔ*              *maá-nnyi*
Crab      he-was  certainly child  stream

11(a) *ne          negiá    a-jyɛ-fyɛ*                 *ula        ne    muú*
however  Crab    he-went-put(Pst)  bottom  with  person

(b) *yi      á-tyɛ́ɛ-ge*                *menyɛέ*
who  he-cooks(RelNonPst)  food

(c) *á-cyɛ́ɛ-ge*                           *meshu*
he-gives(RelNonPst) (to)  Elephant

12(a) *a-ké*
he-said(Pst)

(b) *á-fyɛ́*            *ŋkale    dɔɔ́*
he-put(ImpImm) pepper  much

4(a) 'He asked people (b) to go and (c) clear his farm. 5(a) They went (b) and did clear a big farm. (c) The farm was really big. 6(a) Then they left (the farm) and (b) returned home. 7(a) Elephant prepared food. (b) He gave it (to people) and (c) asked them (d) to eat. 8 They ate a lot of food. 9(a) Elephant shared the food, (but) (b) he did not give any to Crab. 10 Crab was then in the stream. 11(a) However, Crab went and connived with the man (b) who cooks food and (c) serves it to Elephant. 12(a) Crab told him (b) to put a lot of pepper in the food'.

A quick survey of the modes used in this extract shows that, except for 4(b) and (c), 5(c), 7(d), 10, 11(b) and (c), and 12(b), the past is used for the events. In this extract, as in others, the past moves the events forward quickly and is central to the development of the plot. However, it is often interrupted by other modes. Such interruptions are usually meant to encode a different type of discourse information. In 5(c), for example, the clause is stative and merely indicates the attributes of the farm. Similarly in 10, we find an existential stative clause. In 4(b) and (c), 7(d), and 12(b) the imperative is used to tell the participants what they should do. In 11(b) and (c) the relative past is used to explain the significance of the participant just introduced. At these points, progress of the plot is temporarily stopped. Once the events start moving again, the past mode is again used.

The past mode has another function in narrative discourse. In an event block where there are two concurrent events, the preparatory event is marked by the past mode, while the main event is marked by nonpast. The following is from text B:

(43) 15(a) *ne*   *bií*   *bí*   *mbɔ*   *mendé*   *a-jií*           *nte*
        but   day   that   one   wife   she-forgot(Pst)   thought

(b)                              *a-ké*
                             she-said(Pst)

(c)                              *a-kpɛ-ne*       *ne uluú*
                             she enters(NonPst) at  night

(d)                              *a-kpá*       *mewɛ*
                             she-carried(Pst)  light

16(a)                         *a-ké*
                        she-said(Pst)

(b)                              *a-jyɛ-ɛ*
                             she-goes(NonPst)

(c) *ŋkpɛɛ́*  *a-pɔ́-sé*                *ne*   *ndeé*  *ula*
   *Ŋkpɛɛ́*  he-had-no-longer(PstNeg)  with  cloth  buttocks

15(a) 'But on that day the wife forgot, (b) and so that (c) as she went in at night (d) she carried a lamp. 16(a) When (b) she entered, (c) *Ŋkpɛɛ́* had no cover on his buttocks'.

In these two examples, there are two sets of events that are more or less concurrent. The decision to go into the room (15b, 16a) is preparatory to the action of going in (15c, 16b). Though the events are concurrent, the decision is encoded in the past whereas the action is encoded in the non-past.

Past is not the mode one would expect in the conclusion of a story. But when it does occur in this part of a text, its function is not to encode an event. Consider the following example taken from a text not in the appendix.

(44) (a) *ɛwí*   *mbɔ*   *ɛ-lɛré*
      that   one   it-showed(Pst)

(b) *ńnó*   *ŋkpɛɛ́*   *a-lu*       *muú*     *refyá*
     that   *Ŋkpɛɛ́*   he-is(Eq)  person  wicked

'This shows that *Ŋkpɛɛ́* is a wicked man'.

This is the concluding section of a story that tells how *Ŋkpɛɛ́* misused his friend's child (the sheep) whom he had taken on a journey. The moral of the story is stated as a conclusion. However, it is not given as a general condition or truth; hence the nonpast mode. The speaker regards the whole story as an event in the past (though the very immediate past), and the past is used. In this case the past conveys its characteristic semantic meaning of reference to completed action.

**3.2.2 The nonpast mode(NonPst).** The nonpast mode is usually associated with the deep structure expository genre. However, it is prominent in many parts of narrative texts, performing specific functions in the introduction, the body (e.g., as a cohesive element in the system of linkage), and the conclusion.

**3.2.2.1 Nonpast in the introduction.** It was noted earlier that participants are usually introduced with stative clauses in which mode distinctions are unimportant. However, participants may also be introduced with action clauses in the nonpast mode. The following example is from a text not included in the appendix:

(45) (a) *gé-o*
      see(Imp)

    (b) *maá mende*   *awu*    *ne*    *á-lú-ó*
       child-man    certain  and  he-is-the-one-who(RelExist)

    (c) *a-kame-ge*         *Atátá   Moŋga*
       he-answers-to(NonPst)  *Atátá  Moŋga*

    (d) *a-kya-a*         *unyɛ*
       he-hoes(NonPst)   yams

    (e) *a-be-ne*         *aló*
       he-dances(NonPst)  sorcery

  (a) 'Listen, (b) there was a certain man. (c) He was called *Atátá Moŋga*. (d) He was a yam farmer and (e) a sorcerer'.

In this extract, clause (a) is part of the speaker-hearer dimension while clause (b) is the setting. The main participant is introduced in general terms in (b). Clauses (c) to (e) tell us more about the man. Clause (c) names him, while the next two clauses characterize him in terms of his activities. This example has demonstrated the use of the nonpast mode to give more information about a participant already introduced. In the following example the same phenomenon is at work:

(46) Nar: 1(a) *ɛkame*  *yɔɔ*
           story   [call for audience response]

    Aud: (b) *yɔɔ*
           [response]

      2(a) *n-cwɔ́-ɔ-gáre*     *genó*
         I-coming-tell(NonPst)  thing

        (b) *yi*     *gé-pyɛ́-gɛ*
           which   it-happened(RelPst)

(c) *ne*    *mekwɛnde*    *á-la-á*               *mbɔ*    *mbaá*
    and    pig             he-remained(RelPst)    like    that

*maŋgo*
place-to-dig

3    *mekwɛnde*    *ebwɔ*    *ne*    *mewe*    *á-nyɛ-ɛ*
    pig             they    and    tortoise    they-eating(NonPst)

*rejeé*
friendship

2(a) 'I am going to tell the reason (b) why a pig has remained (c) a digger of the earth with his mouth. 3 Pig and tortoise are friends'.

In 3 nonpast is used to give more information about the participants and to establish the situation. The situation, which is created for the audience in order to make it favorable to the events of the main part, is that the pig and the tortoise are friends, and that the tortoise could go to the pig for a loan. This situation, apart from telling something about the participants, also arouses the audience's interest by creating suspense. The audience knows that the tortoise is a trickster and it is not safe to befriend him.

**3.2.2.2 Nonpast as a linkage device.** One of the functions of the nonpast mode is to link the major parts of a discourse. In text B, for example, the introduction is linked to the preparatory episodes by events expressed in the nonpast mode. Similarly, the bridge between the preparatory and the main episode is established by the nonpast mode. Figure 14 shows the plot structure of text B. (Notice the use of the nonpast in 5 and 28.)

**3.2.2.3 Nonpast for climactic events.** While the mode for normal events in an episode is past, the events that lead up to the main event (climax) are marked by nonpast. In text B, the climax of the first episode comes with the wife's discovery of her husband's defect and her threat to divorce him. The climactic action in this part is her decision to abandon her husband as a result of that knowledge. This comes in 18(b) and is encoded in the nonpast.

In the second episode, the climax is *Ŋkpeé*'s attempts to outwit his wife, by which she is completely taken in. The climax of all these actions of deception comes with his actions of cutting, which are expressed in the nonpast.

Another use of the nonpast in the event line is in the expression of concurrent events, one of which is preparatory and the other is main. The main event is expressed in the nonpast mode.

| OUTLINE | NOS. | DISCOURSE INFORMATION | MODE |
|---|---|---|---|
| Introduction | 1–4 | Speaker-hearer relation, 1–3(a) | |
| | | Introduction, 3(b)-(c) | |
| | | Situation, 4 | |
| Link | 5 | Passage of time, 5(a)-(c) | Nonpast |
| Episode 1 (preparatory) | 6–27 | First set of events: | |
| | | *Ŋkpɛɛ́* gives laws to his wife, 6–12 | |
| | | Second set of events: | |
| | | *Ŋkpɛɛ́* drinks and gets drunk, 13(a)-(c) | |
| | | Explanation by the narrator: | |
| | | Why the laws were given, 14(a)-(f) | |
| | | Third set of events: | |
| | | Wife breaks the laws and discovers her husband's defects, 15–19 | |
| | | Fourth set of events: | |
| | | Wife threatens divorce and is appeased, 20–27 | |
| Link | 28 | Repeated appeasement, 28(a)-(d) | Nonpast |
| Episode 2 (main) | 29–48 | First set of events: | |
| | | Further quarrels; wife decides to divorce, 29–32 | |
| | | Second set of events: | |
| | | The husband disguises himself and overtakes her, 33–38 | |
| | | Third set of events: | |
| | | *Ŋkpɛɛ́* outwits the wife, 39–48 | |
| Conclusion | 49 | Speaker-hearer relation, 49(d) | |
| | | Explanation 49(b)-(d) | |

Fig. 14. Plot structure of text B

**3.2.2.4 Nonpast for nonevents.** Nonpast is the mode a speaker uses to make explanations and comments on events in a narrative. It is this information that clarifies the discourse, as illustrated by the following extract from a text:

(47) 28(a) *a-ké*
      she-said(Pst)

    (b) *a-pɔ́*
      he is not

  29(a) *a-tané*
      he-left(Pst)

    (b) *a-wilé*
      he-returned(Pst)

  30(a) *jyɛ́é    ndé    bií    ne    á-cw-ɔ́*
      every   what   day   and   he-who-came(RelPst)

    (b) *ɛbwɔ́     á-abɔ́-ɔ           mbe*
      them that   they-who-take(RelNonPst)   first

    (c) *á-gé-ne         ji*
      they-see(RelNonPst)   him

    (d) *a-ŋma-a       amu*
      she-hangs(NonPst)   hands

    (e) *mmyɛké   a-kwɔ-ɔ      ŋ́kálé*
      as if      she-grinds(NonPst)   pepper

    (f) *wi     ntaá   né   ŋ́kále   pɔ́*
      in-fact  stone   for   pepper   is-not

    (g) *menɔ   wuí   ne   á-bwɔ́le-ge        mbɔ*
      husband  her   that   she-turns(RelNonPst)   like-that

  28(a) 'She said (b) he was not in there. 29(a) He left and (b) went back home. 30(a) Whenever he came, (b) they were the first (c) to see him. (d) She pretends (e) that she is grinding pepper (f) though, in fact, it is not a grinding stone, (g) but the husband that she turns on his back...'

In this extract, 28 and 29 are part of the event-line. In 30(a)-(g), the speaker leaves the event-line to explain that the stone on which the woman is grinding pepper is not, in reality, a grinding stone; it is the tortoise (the husband) that is lying on his back. The wife is merely deceiving the pig because the husband does not want to pay back the money he borrowed from the pig. It will be noticed that the verbs in the explanations are nonpast.

The narrator, in addition to reporting events and giving explanations to clarify them, may also tell his feelings about them. In the text from which the preceding extract is taken, for instance, comments about women in general are made by a male participant who believes that women are usually disobedient. He wants his wife not to disobey the order he gave her not to dig a certain yam. At this point, the narrator breaks in to agree with the male participant that women really are disobedient: *ne wáwálé andé á-kpele-ge makpele* 'but truly women they-disobey(NonPst) orders'. This is an example of a narrator-listener relationship.

**3.2.2.5 Nonpast in the conclusion.** The conclusion of a narrative gives opportunity for the speaker to explain to the hearers the meaning of the story as a whole. Text A is an example. In A26, the elephant's dying near a stream is explained. It is the belief that an elephant must die only near a stream, regardless of where it is shot. In A27(b) and (c) a further explanation is given, i.e., the elephant wants people to have water to drink when it is being butchered.

**3.2.3 The imperative mode.** In chapter 6 it is demonstrated that the imperative is the mode for the deep-structure hortatory genre. In a narrative text, imperative is used in the introduction and conclusion to establish the speaker-hearer relationship. In the body of the text, it is used in direct speech, which forms part of an embedded text.

In chapter 2, it has been shown that the imperative has a number of forms. The form used here is the second person which encodes commands or instructions.

Use of imperative in this connection is related to role structure, which is discussed above. The participant who is the aggressor, the one who initiates moves (actions), gives a command without any modifying words. In text A, for example, Crab becomes the aggressor, the revenger. He ignores Elephant's demand for water and orders Duiker, Elephant's messenger, to go back and inform his master that there is no water.

(48) 21(a) *manaá    mimbɔ    má-pɔ́*
          water    that    it-not(AttrNeg)

   (b) *có-gáré           ji*
       go-tell(ImpImm)    him

  (a) 'There is no water for him, (b) go and tell him'.

Crab is acting from a position of strength. The function of the imperative here is to initiate a new set of actions in which the roles are bound to change. In this particular example, Crab's haughty manner receives a sharp reaction from Elephant, who feels slighted.

Other examples where the imperative mode is used to show that a participant is acting from a position of superiority are found in text B. In B7(e),

*Ŋkpɛé,* as the lawgiver, warns his wife to knock at the door whenever she wants to come in.

**3.2.4 The relative modes.** The function of the relative modes is to further identify the character. One characteristic of the relative modes — both relative past and nonpast — in a narrative discourse is to characterize an action as to whether it is a specific or a general condition. If an action is a specific condition, the relative nonpast (RelNonPst) is used.

Examples of relative past in text A include 24(d) and (e). From the same text, general conditions are expressed in 11(b) and (c). If 11(b) and 20(b) are compared with 20(c), the distinction between actions denoting general conditions and those denoting specific conditions will become clear.

(49) A11(a) *ne*           *negiá*   *a-jyɛ-fyé*         *ula*     *me*   *muú*
              however   Crab   he-went-put(Pst)   bottom   with   per-
    son

    (b) *yi*    *á-tyéɛ-ge*            *menyɛé*
        who   he-cooks(RelNonPst)   food

    (c) *á-cyéɛ-ge*           *meshu*
        he-gives(RelNonPst) (to)   Elephant

   (a) 'However, Crab went and connived with the man (b) who cooks food and (c) serves it to Elephant'.

In text A, 11(b) and (c), the actions of cooking for and giving food to Elephant are characterized as habitual or general in condition. They are not single events with specified boundaries.

Consider now A20(b) and (c):

(50) A20(b) *átá meshu*     *yi*    *á-nyɛ-é*       *menyɛé*
             Papa Elephant   who   he-ate(RelPst)   food

    (c) *á-nyo-mé*           *me*
        he-(who)-refused(RelPst)   me

   (b) 'Is it Papa Elephant who ate food (c) and refused to give me some?'

The action is a specific event or circumstance. It is marked here by the relative past.

**3.2.5 The aspectual modes.** The three aspectual modes, namely, repetitive (Rep), inceptive (Incep), and habitual (Hab), have specific functions in a narrative text.

**3.2.5.1 The repetitive mode.** The repetitive aspect usually indicates repetition of an action. In narrative discourse, it has both anaphoric (pointing backward) and cataphoric (pointing forward) meaning and occurs with preparatory events. Anaphoric meaning derives from the fact that a former action is repeated. For example, in text B, this mode occurs in 10(a) to show that the laws were given repeatedly, in 29(a) for a repeat of a quarrel, and in 38(b) for a repeat of a deception. These occurrences are anaphoric because 10(a) points backward to an earlier action in 6 and 7, and 38(b) points to a similar action in 33(e). Cataphoric meaning is seen in the fact that this is the beginning of a new set of events.

**3.2.5.2 The inceptive mode.** The inceptive aspect normally marks an action as recently started, but in a narrative text its function is to mark the focal point or climax of a set of events. In B13(d), for example, after giving the laws and getting drunk, Ŋkpɛɛ́ goes to sleep. His sleep is seen as crucial, leading to a change of the role structure. In the same text, the inceptive in 33(e) indicates the climax of a set of disguised actions started in 33(a). Similarly, in 38(f), we find the climax of another set of disguise actions started in 38(a).

**3.2.5.3 The habitual mode.** The habitual aspect in a narrative text marks the result of a series of events and occurs in the conclusion. The following example from the conclusion of a text (not in appendix B) shows the final result of the events of a story:

(51) *mekwɛnde*   *a-la-la*                *yɛ́*      *meno*      *mme*
     Pig              he-Hab-remained(Pst)   then      mouth      down

    'From that time Pig continues to dig the earth with his snout'.

### 3.3 Summary

In this chapter it is demonstrated that verb forms (or modes) in Dényá narrative discourse are related to the structure of text. Some of the modes characterize narrative material either as backbone (event-line) or as elaborative and supportive. Figure 15 summarizes the functions of the modes discussed in this chapter.

Events in a narrative are not all of the same significance. The most significant events are the climactic ones, which are marked by the nonpast mode. The events that are preparatory to climactic ones form the greater part of the event-line and are marked by the past. There are also different types of non events, as the chart shows.

The uses of the past and nonpast modes are summarized as follows:

Past

(1) The past is the principal mode for the event-line. Its function is to advance the discourse. Statistically, it is the most frequent mode in nar-

| DISCOURSE INFORMATION | SPECIFICATION | MODE |
|---|---|---|
| EVENTS | Preparation | Past Repetitive aspect |
| | Climax | Nonpast Inceptive aspect |
| | Resolution | Nonpast |
| NONEVENTS | Explanation, Conclusion | Nonpast |
| | Identification of participants | Nonpast |
| | (a) Specific condition | Relative past |
| | (b) General condition | Relative nonpast |
| | Speaker-hearer relationship | Imperative |
| | Result, Conclusion | Habitual aspect |
| | Linkage | Nonpast |

Fig. 15. Summary of the modes in narrative discourse

rative text. It does not normally occur in the introduction or conclusion.

(2) It is the mode for marking events preparatory to the climax and its resolution.

(3) When used to state the moral of a story, it indicates the obvious conclusion to be drawn from the narration.

Nonpast

(1) Nonpast is used with reference to characters already introduced, characterizing them in terms of their activities or some relationship.

(2) It is used as a linkage device, marking the transition from one major part of discourse to another, e.g., from introduction to preparatory episode, or from preparatory episode to climactic episode.

(3) Within an episode, it marks climactic events.

(4) It indicates the main event of two concurrent events.

(5) It is used to give background information and comments.

(6) It is used to give the moral in a conclusion.

# 4 Modes in Procedural Discourse

A Dényá speaker uses procedural discourse to describe habitual activities such as work processes, ceremonies, or festivals that are carried out repeatedly in very much the same way. He uses procedural discourse also to give the steps in a particular process such as extracting palm oil, weaving a sleeping mat, or distilling the local gin *afɔfɔ*. A procedural text may be embedded in a narrative or other kind of text.

Unlike narrative discourse, which has an agent-event orientation, a procedural discourse is goal-oriented with object focus. However, like the narrative, it is ordered chronologically. In terms of the time dimension, a narrative is in accomplished time, while procedural discourse is in projected time. Longacre (1968, 1976) notes that projected time is encoded by some form of nonpast tense and quite often by future tense. But in Dényá, where there is no future tense in surface structure, projected time is still encoded by the past mode (see sec. 4.2).

One of the parameters Longacre uses to distinguish discourse genres is person-orientation. A Dényá procedural discourse could be in the 1st, 2nd, or 3rd person. If a speaker wants to identify himself with the particular activity, he uses the 1st person (see text C in the appendix), but usually the 2nd person singular is the most natural. Nearly all the procedural texts used for this study are in the 2nd person singular.

## 4.1 The Internal Structure of a Procedural Text

A Dényá procedural text, like a narrative, consists of introduction, body, and conclusion. The texts analysed for this study were response monologues; that is, they were elicited by asking for a given procedure. The speaker assumes that the hearer does not know the procedure being described.

**4.1.1 Introduction.** The introduction of a procedural discourse is much more limited in scope than that of a narrative. Its only feature is the speaker-hearer relationship, which includes the opening and topic.

The most natural opening of an introduction in the language is a hypothetical condition in the first clause with the topic established in the following
clause. Text C gives a clear example.

(52) 1(a) *mbɔgé*      *n-jɔɔ́-gé*
         if          I-said(Cond)

     (b) *ńnó*      *n-cwɔ-ɔ-jó*              *gébɔ̌*
         that       I-come-weave(NonPst)      mat

     (c) *n-kpɛ*              *mewaá*
         I-entered(Pst)      forest

(a) 'If I decided (b) to weave a sleeping mat, (c) I would go into the forest'.

Clause 1(a) is the opening of the discourse. The question that elicited this
text was, "What would you do if you wanted to make a sleeping mat?" The
question suggests the topic of the discourse: "Making a sleeping mat," which
the speaker states in 1(b). It is the goal; it is the primary focus. Once stated,
the topic is hardly mentioned again until the conclusion when the final goal
is attained.

It is important to note that in most of the texts analysed, the discourse topic
is the same as the episode topic since most texts are single-episode texts. As
a discourse advances, subtopics are established, and once established, a subtopic is seldom named until a new subtopic is introduced. Text C clearly illustrates this point. The new subtopic, "getting and preparing the material,"
is introduced in 1(d). The reed used is named in 1(d) and is not named again
until 9, where it has been transformed into another state. However,
pronominal reference to it is made in 1(f) and 2(e).

A text (not in the appendix) that gives the procedure for distilling the local
gin *afɔ́fɔ́* is an example of one containing two episodes. The first episode
deals with the production of palm wine; the second gives the steps involved
in using the palm wine to produce the gin. Each episode begins with a
hypothetical condition. The following are the opening sentences of the two
episodes:

(53) (a) *mbɔgé*      *ɔ-jɔɔ́-gé*
         if          you-decided(Cond)

     (b) *ńnɔ́*      *ɔ-jyɛ-ɛ-tyéɛ*              *afɔ́fɔ́*
         that       you-go-cook(NonPst)        gin

     'If you decided that you were going to distill the local gin . . .'

(54) (a) *ɔ-jɔɔ́-gé*                      *yɛ́*
         you-decided(Cond)       then

(b) *nnó   ɔ-cwɔ-ɔ-tyéɛ*                    *afɔfɔ*
    that   you-come-cook(NonPst)   gin

'If you have decided then that you are about to distill the wine into gin . . .'

In 53 we have the introduction to the discourse which states the discourse topic, the making of gin. In 54 we find an episode introduction; the focus is on distilling the palm wine that was produced in the first episode.

**4.1.2 Body.** The body, or main part, of a procedural text may consist of one or more episodes, but quite often, Dényá procedural texts are single-episode discourses. An episode usually develops step-by-step the topic announced in the introduction. The act is a set of preparatory and main actions and may include the result of actions. In terms of their functions in plots, the acts may be classified as prepeak, peak, or postpeak (dénouement). The prepeak actions are preparatory to the peak ones; peak actions result in the finished product; and postpeak actions indicate what happens to the finished product.

The body of a procedural discourse is similar to that of a narrative. Chapter 3 shows a narrative as a sequence of events, actions within a given time span. In procedural texts, the main feature is a step-by-step sequence of actions, with one step being completed before another is begun. The overall time setting is not particularly significant as it is in a narrative. In both procedural and narrative discourse, certain actions are preparatory and others are main ones.

Figure 16 is an analysis of the internal structure of a 2nd-person monologue, "Making a sleeping mat." (Text C in appendix B treats the same subject but in the 1st person.)

In the text analysed in figure 16, the speaker is describing how to weave a sleeping mat, a job done only by women. The introduction consists of clauses 1(a–d), and the body is made up of six acts. The first act includes getting the materials from the forest and drying them. The preparatory actions are getting the reed from the forest, bringing it home, removing its thorns, and spreading it out in the sun to dry. The main action is the drying. In fact, subsequent actions are dependent upon this. But the process of drying is omitted because the action is not performed by a human agent. After the reed has been spread out in the sun, what is noticed is the result, which is that the material becomes dry. For the same reasons, the main actions are omitted in act 3; that is, whitening, like the drying of the material, is done by the sun.

| OUTLINE | SPECIFICATIONS | CONTENT |
|---|---|---|
| INTRODUCTION | Initiation of procedure | Decision to weave a sleeping mat |
| (1) | (1a-d) | Going to the forest |
| BODY (2-21) | Act 1 (2-7) | Getting the material and drying it |
| | Material defined (background) (2-3) | Reed that grows in water or on land |
| | Preparatory actions (4-6) | Removing thorns Drying in the sun |
| | Result (7) | Reed is dried |
| | Act 2 (8-10) | Softening of material |
| | Course A | |
| | Preparatory actions (8a) | Getting the softener |
| | Main actions | Softening |
| | Course B | |
| | Preparatory actions (9a) | Building a beam for softening |
| | Main action | Softening |
| | Result (10) | It is soft |
| | Act 3 (11-12) | Whitening the material |
| | Preparatory (11) | Spreading the material in the sun |
| | Result (12) | Whitened material |
| | Act 4 (13-16) | Preparing for weaving |

| OUTLINE | SPECIFICATIONS | CONTENT |
|---|---|---|
| | Preparatory (13-14) | Splitting the material |
| | Main action (15-16) | Dyeing the material |
| | Act 5 (17-19) | Climax: Actual weaving |
| | Preparatory (17a) | Adding white design |
| | Main (17b-18b) | Colored design |
| | Result (19) | Complete mat |
| | Act 6 (20-21) | Dénouement |
| | Preparatory (20-21a) | Hemming the mat |
| | Result | Finished product |
| CONCLUSION (22-23) | Speaker-hearer relationship (22) | |
| | Restatement of topic (23) | That is how we weave a sleeping mat |

Fig. 16. Internal structure of the procedural text,
"How to Weave a Sleeping Mat"

In act 2, two courses are opened to the listener as regards the method of softening the reed:

(55) 8(a) *é-dɛ-gé*
(if when) it-dried(Cond)

(b) *ɔ́-bɔ́*            *gempeé*
you-took(NonPst)   bamboo

(c) *ɔ-pwɛa-ge*        *wíɛ*
you-soften(NonPst)   with it

(d) ɔ-pwɛa-ge
you-soften(NonPst)

(e) ɔ-pwɛa-ge
you-soften(NonPst)

9(a) wɔ    yifɔ     á-wé              wɔ    genɔ́   mbale
    you   another   they-tied(NonPst)   you   stick   veranda

(b) ɔ-su-u                wié
you-scrape(NonPst)    there

(c) ɔ-su-u
you-scrape(NonPst)

(d) ɔ-su-u
you-scrape(NonPst)

10(a) ɔ-su-gé
if you-scraped(Cond)

(b) é-pwɛa
it-became-soft(Pst)

8(a) 'When it is dry, (b) you take a piece of bamboo and (c-e) soften the reed with it.

9(a) For another woman, a beam is erected at the veranda (b-d) on which she scrapes it.

10(a) When you have scraped it, (b) it becomes soft'.

The first course of action is given in 8 and the second in 9. Whichever course is preferred, it consists of preparatory and main actions and the result is the same: the reed becomes soft.

Act 4 gives the actions immediately preceding the actual weaving of the mat; that is, splitting the material into "males," which are longer, and "females," which are shorter. This act does not have the element of result.

Act 5 is the climax, and it includes three elements: preparatory, main and result. Earlier acts are preparatory to the weaving of the mat.

Act 6 is a type of dénouement. The hearer is informed that the weaving is completed. The hemming of the edges is preparatory to the main action of lying on it. It is now a finished product.

**4.1.3 Conclusion.** As in narrative texts, conclusions of procedural texts have the speaker-hearer dimension, and the topic is repeated. The text that figure 16 is based on ends as follows:

(56) 22(a) *gé*                        *mbɔ*
        see(ImpImm)    like-that

    (b) *ne*    *á-jo-me*                    *gebɔ*
        and    they-weave(NonPst)    mat

'See, that is how a mat is woven'.

In this example, (22a) directly draws the attention of the hearer to the steps given in the discourse, and in (b) the topic is restated, but in general terms. Throughout the discourse the speaker says "You do this; you do that," but in the conclusion he changes to the more impersonal form—a form translated into the passive in English.

### 4.2 The Use of Modes in Procedural Discourse

The close similarity of the internal structure of narrative and procedural texts is reflected in the use of verb forms. The selection and function of the modes appear identical in many places. However, there are differences.

**4.2.1 The conditional mode.** The conditional mode is unimportant in narrative discourse, but in procedural discourse it plays a significant role, as seen in text C:

(57) 1(a) *mbɔgé*    *n-jɔ́-gé*
       if        I-said(Cond)

    (b) *ńnó*    *n-cwɔ-ɔ-jó*                *gébɔ̌*
        that    I-come-weave(NonPst)    mat

    (c) *ŋ-kpɛ*            *mewaá*
        I-entered(Pst)    forest

    (d) *n-sɔ́*        *ŋkó*
        I-cut(Pst)    reed

    (e) *ŋ-kpá*
        I-carried(Pst)

    (f) *n-cwɔ́*        *ne*    *éj´i*    *mmu*
        I-came(Pst)    with    it        home

  2(a) *n-cwɔ-gé*
       I-came(Cond)

    (b) *m-feé*            *meshií*
        I-removed(Pst)    thorns

    (c) *m-feé*
        I-removed(Pst)

    (d) *m-feé*
       I-removed(Pst)

    (e) *ŋ-kpá*         *yɛ*    *éjʹi*
       I-carried(Pst)   then   it

    (f) *ŋm-ŋme*      *ŋm-ŋmɛé*
       I-threw(Pst)   sun

  3(a)      *ŋm-ŋme-gé*     *ŋm-ŋmɛé*
      (if)   I-threw(Cond)   sun

    (b) *é-kpéa*
       they-whiten(Attr)

  4(a)      *é-kpɛá-gé*       *yé*
      (if)   they-whiten(Cond)   then

    (b) *m̃-bɔ́*      *anɔ*
       I-took(Pst)   males

    (c) *ŋ̌-gyá*
       I-split(Pst)

    (d) #  *agiɛ́*
       females

    (e) *ŋ̌-gyá*
       I-split(Pst)

1(a) 'If I decided (b) to weave a sleeping mat, (c) I would go into the forest, (d) cut reed, (e) and carry it (f) home.

2(a) Having come home, (b-d) I would remove the thorns, (e) carry it out, (f) and spread it in the sun.

3(a) Spread in the sun, (b) the material becomes white.

4(a) When it is white, (b-c) I split it into males (d-e) and females'.


   The conditional mode appears in 1(a), 3(a), and 4(a). The question is, What is the function of this mode in the text? Its primary function is to provide the linkage mechanism; it is the logical link with the question which elicited the text.

   It should be recognized that 1-3 constitute one act, and that 4 is the beginning of a new one. 1 and 2 are the preparatory actions of this act; C3 is the result. The conditional mode is used to link one set of completed and closely related actions with another. Though 1 and 2 are preparatory actions in the act, they are quite distinct activities—one set must be finished before the other begins. There is normally a time lapse between the end of 1 and the beginning of 2.

The formal linguistic device for marking a chain of completed distinct actions is the conditional mode. What is interesting about this is the fact that the link, itself a clause, is a repeat of the verb of the preceding clause. Longacre (1968, 1976) refers to this phenomenon as "tail-head linkage." Thus 2(a) repeats the verb in 1(f), 3(a) repeats the verb in 2(f), and 4(a) repeats the verb in 3(b). This system of linkage is another formal difference between narrative and procedural discourse.

**4.2.2 The past mode.** The past mode indicates a preparatory action rather than a main action or result. Each action given in the past mode anticipates another one to follow it. Its function is to develop the plot, a function it performs also in narratives. In the preceding extract from text C (in sec. 4.2.1), after the introduction, 1(a-b), the body of the discourse is marked by the past mode. In the first act, the preparatory actions, which continue through 2(f), are all given in the past mode. When this mode is interrupted by the occurrence of another mode, different discourse information is expected.

**4.2.3 The nonpast mode.** The nonpast mode has a number of functions in procedural discourse. Normally, preparatory actions, which are marked by the past mode, lead to main ones, which are nonpast, unless there is reason to the contrary as shown earlier. Thus, one use of the nonpast is to mark an activity as the main one in the process. The following extract is episode 1 from a text on distilling gin.

(58) 1(a) *mbɔgé*     *ɔ-jɔɔ́-gé*
       if           you-decided(Cond)

    (b) *ńnó*    *ɔ-jyɛ-ɛ-tyɛ́ɛ*         *afɔ́fɔ́*
       that    you-go-cook(NonPst)    local gin

    (c) *gé*
       see(ImpImm)

    (d) *ŋkane*     *ɔ́-pyɛ́-ɛ*
       how       you-do(RelNonPst)

   2(a) *ɔ́-fɛ́*             *mewaá*
       you-went(Pst)    forest

    (b) *ɔ́-kɛ*           *undiá*
       you-felled(Pst)    palms

   3(a)      *ɔ-kɛ-gé*          *undiá*
       (if)    you-felled(Cond)    palms

    (b)    *á-belé-gé*         *nelɔ*   *éni*
        (if)    they-slept(Cond)   days   four

    (c) *ɔ́-fέ*
       you-went(Pst)

    (d) *ɔ́-pwá*
       you-pruned(Pst)

4(a)       *ɔ-pwá-gé*
       (if)   you-pruned(Cond)

    (b) *ɔ́-taré*
       you-attached(Pst) receptacles

5   *ɔ-cɛne-ge*         *dondo*    *ne*   *ŋkwale*
   you-tap(NonPst)    morning   and   evening

6(a) *ɔ́ké*
      you-said(Pst)

    (b) *ɔ-cɛne-ge*     *mbɔ*
       you-tap(NonPst)   like-that

    (c) *mmɔɔ́*   *má-tané-ge*
       wine      it-comes-out(NonPst)

7(a)      *mmɔɔ́*   *má-tané-gé*
       (if)   wine    it-comes-out(Cond)

    (b) *ɔ́-feré*
       you-removed(Pst)

    (c) *ɔ́-fané*         *ne*   *genó gifɔ́*   *kpaa*
       you-poured(Pst)   into   thing (Indef)   big

The nonpast occurs in 1(b), 5, and 6(b,c). In this episode, the main action is the producing of palm wine. Going to the forest in 2(a), felling palms in 2(b), pruning the felled palms in 3(d), and attaching the receptacles in 4(b), are all preparatory actions since they do not really produce wine. It is when the palms are tapped that the wine comes out and is collected. Tapping the palms in 5 is the main action, and it is marked by the nonpast mode.

In the same text, the climax of the second episode is marked by the nonpast. Compare this with the use of nonpast in narrative discourse, where main events are given in the nonpast mode. In extract (58), the function of nonpast in 1(b) is seen in relation to 1(a), which is a preparatory action, or setting for the main action, the distilling process, which is given in the nonpast.

It should also be noted that in 1(b) the topic of the discourse is stated. In other words, the nonpast is used to state the topic. The restatement of the topic in the conclusion is also in this mode. The following, from a text that gives the procedure for preparing a certain vegetable, is an example of such a restatement of the topic in the conclusion:

(59) 2(a)        ɔ-sɔ-gé       ŋkó
       (if)    you-cut(Cond)   reed

    (b) ŋkó  yi  mbɔ  ɛ-cû-ge        mewaá  sé
        reed  that  one  it-grows(NonPst)  forest  our

    (c) ɛyífɔ́    é-cû-ge          nnyi
        some    it-grows(NonPst)  (in)-stream

    (d) ɛ-yífɔ́   é-cû-ge          mewaá
        some    it-grows(NonPst)  (in)-forest

2(a) 'When you want to cut reed, (b) reed (that I'm talking about) grows in the forest, (c) some grows in water, (d) some grows on land...'

In this part of the text the speaker makes an explanation — some background information about the material to be used. He states that the reed is found in their forest and that it grows either in streams or on land. This, of course, is a general truth, which every Anya man knows. It is not, therefore, surprising that this part of the text is encoded in the nonpast, both as a general truth and as an explanation.

Similarly, the dénouement usually gives what happens to the finished product and is, therefore, a general truth. In this text on the preparation of a vegetable is found a good example of a dénouement:

(60) (a) bɔɔ́      á-la-bɔ́
      people   they-Hab-took(Pst)

    (b) á-nyɛ-ɛ            wíɛ
      they-eat(NonPst)  (along)  with-it

    (a) 'People then take it and (b) eat it (with something else)'.

To summarize, then, the nonpast mode in a procedural text encodes main actions, states or restates topics, and states general truths.

**4.2.4. The imperative mode.** The imperative mode indicates the speaker-hearer relationship in both introductions and conclusions. The use of the imperative is not to encode injunctions. Its use can be seen in the following extract from a text on making gin:

(61) 1(a) mbɔgé   ɔ-jɔ́-gé
       if       you-said(Cond)

(b) *ńnó*    *ɔ-jyɛ-ɛ-tyɛ́ɛ*              *afɔ́fɔ́*
that    you-go-cook(NonPst)    gin

(c) *gé*
see(ImpImm)

(d) *ŋkane*    *ɔ́-pyɛ́-ɛ*
how    you-do(RelNonPst)

27(a)        *a-kwené-gé*
(if)    it-cooled(Cond)

(b) *bɔɔ́*        *á-la nyú*
people    they-Hab-drank(Pst)

28(a) *gé*                    *mbɔ*
see(ImpImm)    like-that

(b) *ne*    *á-pyɛ́-ɛ*                    *afɔ́fɔ́*
that    they-make(RelNonPst)    gin

1 (a) 'If you wanted (b) to distill the local gin, (c) see, (d) this is how you go about it.

27(a) When it is cooled, (b) people drink it.

28(a) That is how (b) the local gin is made'.

Example 62 is from a text on preparing *gélú*, a vegetable:

(62) 1(a) *gé*
see(ImpImm)

(b) *nduge*    *ɛsé*    *bɔɔ́*    *Anyá*    *de-tyɛɛ-ge*              *gélú*
as    we    people    Anya    we-prepare(NonPst)    vegetable

26(a) *bɔɔ́*        *á-la-bɔ́*
people    they-Hab-took(Pst)

(b) *á-nyɛ-ɛ*                    *wiɛ́*
they-eat(NonPst)    (along with) it

27(a) *gé*                    *mbɔ*
see(ImpImm)    like-that

(b) *ne*    *ɛsé*    *de-tyɛ́ɛ-ge*              *gélú*
and    we    we-prepare (RelNonPst)    vegetable

1 (a) This is how (b) the Anya people prepare *gélú*.

26(a) People take it and (b) eat it (along with something else).

27(a) That is how (b) we prepare *gélú*.

In examples 61 and 62 the first sentence in each is the introduction, while 27 and 28 in 61 and 26 and 27 in 62 form the conclusions of their respective texts. In 61 the imperative mode is used in 1(c) and 28(a), and in 62 this mode is used in 1(a) and 27(a). In each case, this mode calls attention to speaker-hearer relationship in the discourse. In the introduction the speaker draws attention to the chain of actions to follow. In the conclusion he once more addresses the hearer directly, expecting that the procedure outlined in the body has been followed. In other words, this mode gives a logical conclusion to what has been given in the body of the discourse.

**4.2.5 The habitual mode.** The habitual mode is used to mark the dénouement, or the final result of the procedure. Usually, the dénouement comprises what happens to the finished product. In examples 61 and 62, the dénouement occurs in 27(b) and 26(a), respectively.

## 4.3 Summary

Five modes feature prominently in Dényá procedural discourse: conditional, past, nonpast, imperative, and habitual. Their functions can be summarized as follows:

(1) The conditional mode provides the head-tail linkage system between the set of actions that make up the procedure.

(2) The past mode is the mode for the procedure-line, as it is for the event-line in narrative discourse. It advances a discourse toward its goal.

(3) The nonpast mode is used to state the topic in both the introduction and the conclusion. Also, it indicates climactic actions, and it is used in stating general truths.

(4) The imperative mode establishes the speaker-hearer relationship in both the introduction and the conclusion.

(5) The habitual aspect mode marks the final result of a procedure. It indicates what happens to the finished product.

# 5 Modes in Expository Discourse

When a speaker of Dényá wants to describe or explain, he uses expository discourse. Expository is a deep-structure genre, as are narrative, procedural, and hortatory (see fig.1). Expository discourse refers to a text or surface structure that encodes the deep structure expository genre. However, in this study it was found that the surface structure of a text whose intention is to explain or describe can contain other genres. Conversely, other discourse genres have been found to have material in their surface structures that can be described as expository in character. In text D, for example, procedural information is encoded in 8(b) to 10. Text N (not in the appendix) encodes hortatory matter in the introduction and in the conclusion. These different genres are clearly marked by the use of the relevant modes.

The expository material of a text, which is isomorphic with the deep-structure expository genre, is subject-matter oriented, which means that interest is centered on what is being described or explained. Expository texts are given mainly in the third person, though other persons are possible. Unlike narrative and, to some extent, procedural discourse, where time is focal, in the expository genre time is nonfocal. This probably explains the high frequency of stative and nonverbal clauses.

## 5.1 The Internal Structure of an Expository Text

Like the texts of other discourse genres, an expository text may be divided into introduction, body, and conclusion. But the introduction and the conclusion are not part of the exposition-line; in other words,they do not contain the deep-structure expository genre.

**5.1.1 Introduction.** The introduction appears to be an optional element. This is suggested by the fact that of the ten texts on which this study is based, only one contains an introduction. Where there is an introduction, it includes only the speaker-hearer relationship and the main topic of the exposition.

In the following extract, sentence 1 serves to establish the speaker-hearer relationship. The speaker calls the hearer "my child" and invites him to where he, the speaker, is. The Dényá know that the addressee is not the speaker's own child because a parent calls his own child by name. The function of this introduction is to establish a degree of intimacy. Sentence 3 expresses the speaker's intention to tell the hearer something, but the topic of the exposition is not announced.

(63) 1    *maá*  *wa,*  *cwɔ́*        *wi*
         child  my  come(ImpImm)  this-way

     2                  *jwɔ́lé*     *ka*
                         sit(ImpImm)  down

     3(a)               *m̀-bɔ́*    *ɛkéké*  *mecɔ*
                      I-have(Pst)  little   thing

       (b)            *manaŋgaré*  *wɔ*
                      to-tell    you

1 'My child, come here.

2 Sit down.

3 (a) I have something (b) to tell you'.

Other texts that do not include the speaker-hearer relationship are response monologues, prompted by a question. Text D, for example, was given when the speaker was asked to imagine a foreigner who does not know what *ŋgbɛ* is. He was asked, "What do you Anya people call *ŋgbɛ*?" In this situation there was no need for a speaker to establish the speaker-hearer relationship; therefore, the topic of the discourse having been suggested, he went straight into his explanation.

**5.1.2 Body.** The body of an expository text consists of argument blocks, and an argument block comprises a topic sentence (ts) and one or more expositions (exp). The topic sentence identifies the subject of an argument block, and expositions are explanations or specifications of what has been stated in the topic sentence. Figure 17 (pg. 68) shows the internal structure of text D.

**5.1.3 Conclusion.** The conclusion, like the introduction, contains the speaker-hearer dimension. In addition, it includes a closure phrase. An example of the former is in D13(a) and of the latter in D13(b).

**5.2 The Use of Modes in Expository Discourse**

Expository discourse differs from other discourse genres in its clause types and, consequently, its verb types. The exposition-line is mainly expounded by stative clauses (i.e., nonverbal predicates). It will be remembered that nonverbal clauses, in narrative as well as in procedural discourse, are not part of

| NOS. | ARGUMENT | BLOCK EXAMPLES |
|------|----------|----------------|
| 1-2 | *Ngbɛ* is an organization for men | ts 1(a)<br>exp 1 1(b) exp 2 1(c)<br>exp 3 2(a) and 2(b) |
| 3-4 | *Ngbɛ* has laws for the good of the society | ts 3(a) and 3(b)<br>exp1 4(a) and 4(b)<br>exp 2 4(c) and 4(d) |
| 5-7 | *Ngbɛ* is a stratified organization | ts 5(a)<br>exp 1 5(b)<br>exp 2 5(c)<br>exp 3 6 to 7 |
| 8-10 | What to do to become a member (Nonexpository; mainly procedural) | |
| 11 | The advantages of being a member | ts 11(a)<br>exp11(b) to (d) |
| 12 | *Ngbɛ* has many aspects | ts 12(a)<br>exp 12(b-d) |
| 13 | Conclusion | Speaker-Hearer 13(a)<br>Closure 13(b) |

Fig. 17. Display of text D

the event or procedure-line and, thus, are peripheral to the discourses. In expository discourse, however, stative clauses are central. In text D, for example, of the twenty-six clauses in the exposition-line, eleven are stative. The following predicates are from text D; in this limited sample, three types of stative clauses are represented.

(64) 1(a) *a-lu lé uka ande* 'it is an organization'   identification

   (c) *á-pɔ́* 'are not'                        identification

   2(a) *a-lu uka* 'it is an organization'       equative

   3(a) *a-wia mabɛ́* 'it has laws'               possessive

Besides stative verbs, one also encounters the nonpast, relative, and conditional verbs in the exposition-line.

**5.2.1 The Nonpast.** In the narrative and procedural genres, nonpast is the mode that indicates main, or climactic, events, as well as background information which is given in the form of explanation. Thus nonpast can be regarded as the characteristic mode of deep structure exposition, since, in any text, explanations are encoded in that mode. Note that stative clauses are also characteristic of expository discourse.

In a purely expository text, nonpast has other definite functions. Consider the following extract (from another text not in appendix B):

(65) 4(a) *gekpo,   genó   yi gé   á-kú-u*                *ńnó*
         poverty  thing  which  they-call(RelNonPst)  that

         *gekpo*
         poverty

   (b) *genó   gé-bo*
       thing  it-bad(Attr)

  5(a)    *ɔ-bɛ-gé*            *gekpo*
        (if) you-are(Cond)  poor

   (b) *ɔ-bɛ-ɛ*              *bɔɔ*     *ame*   *fúú*
       you-are(NonPst)  people  eyes  open

   (c) *né   ɛcomele   ɛwíɛ   mɛó   muú,*
       in  a gathering  your  speech  person

       *ǎ-fyé-é*             *mekpo  wié*
       he-put-not(NonPst)  head  where

  6(a) *muú   gekpo,   andé   á-kíí*                  *ji*
       person  poor,  woman  they-love-not(NonPstNeg)  him

   (b) *mendé   a-lu         mbɔ*
       woman  she-is(Attr)  like-that

   (c)     *a-kɛle-ge*          *ŋka*
         she-wants(NonPst)  money

   (d)     *a-kɛle-ge*          *mandeé*
         she-wants(NonPst)  clothes

   (e)     *a-kɛle-ge*          *ndé   ndé*
         she-wants(NonPst)  what  not

  7(a)     *ɔ-bɛ-gé*            *gekpo*
        (if)  you-are(Cond)  poor

   (b) *ɔ́-ká-gé-fyé*                      *maá*      *ne*  *mwɛ*
       you-know-not-put(NonPstNeg)  children  in  school

   (c) *nwɛ      a-kɛle-ge*           *ŋka*
       schooling  it-requires(NonPst)  money

8(a)        *maá*   *a-bɛ-gé*          *wɔ*     *nwɛ*
    (if)    child   he-be(Cond)       you      school

  (b)                *ɔ-cyɛɛ-ge*              *ji*      *ŋka*     *nwɛ*
                     you-give(NonPst)         him      money    school

  (c)                *ɔ-cyɛɛ-ge*              *ji*      *mandeé*
                     you-give(NonPst)         him      clothes

  (d) *ɔ-cyɛɛl-ge*           *ji*     *ŋka*       *meyɛé*
      you-give(NonPst)       him      money       food

9(a)            *ɔ́-lá-pɔ́*                      *ne*       *ŋka*
                you(it)-not(AttrNeg)           with      money

  (b)           *ɔ́-pyɛ́-ɛ́*                       *ébi-na*
                you-not-do(NonPstNeg)           these-things

4(a) 'Poverty, what is called poverty, (b) is a bad thing.

5(a) If you are poor, (b) you are worthless in people's eyes; (c) in a gathering nobody listens to what you say.

6(a) A poor man is not loved by women; (b) a woman normally is like this: (c) she requires money, (d) she wants clothes, and (e) she needs many other things.

7(a) If you are poor, (b) you will not be able to send your children to school. (c) Schooling requires money.

8(a) If you have a child in school, (b) you give him school fees, (c) you give him clothes, (d) you give him money for food.

9(a) If you don't have money, (b) you can't do any of these'.

The foregoing text is an expository text on poverty. Though it may include deep-structure hortatory discourse in that it is intended to influence the addressee's attitude, the surface structure is an expository text par excellence.

A close study of the extract above shows that the nonpast mode is used in 5(b) and (c), 6(a) and (c-e), 7(b-c), 8(b-d), and 9(b). The question to ask is, What function does this mode perform in these examples? It has been seen that nonpast encodes general conditions or characteristics. In this connection, it is also the mode for expressing general truths. In 5(c), for example, it is observed that a general characteristic or condition of this society, perhaps also of all others, is that what a poor man says is never valued. In 6(a), it is considered a general characteristic of women not to love poor men. Again, women are characterized in 6(c-e) in terms of what they usually require. In 7(b-c) and 8(b-d), as well as 9(b), the conditions are given as general truths.

It is a truth that a school child needs money for clothes and food, and it is also true that a man without money cannot provide these.

In text D, examples in which the nonpast is used to encode general truths are 1(b) and 12(d). In the former, it is a general truth that nonmembers are not allowed into the organization. Similarly, in the latter, it is a general truth that membership in *Ngbɛ* gives right to free entry into the organization outside your own village.

**5.2.2 The relative modes.** Both the relative past and the relative nonpast are used in expository text. However, it is the latter that is more frequently employed. Text D contains several examples:

(66) 2(a)  *ŋgbɛ*      *a-lu*           *uka*
          *Ngbe*      it-is(Attr)      organization

    (b) *bí*        *ú-kwyɛ́ɛ-ge*                *melɔ*
        which      it-makes-good(RelNonPst)    village

    3(a)            *a-wia*          *mabɛ́*
                   it-has(Attr)     laws

    (b) *yí*        *á-pyɛ́-ɛ*                   *melɔ*
        which      they-make(RelNonPst)       village

    (c)             *ɛ́-kɛ́-ne*                  *cáncá*
                   it-moves(RelNonPst)        well

    4(a) *jyɛɛ́*     *ɔ-lu*              *wiɛ́*
         even-if    you-are(Attr)      there

    (b) *jyɛí*      *ɔ-pɔ́*              *wiɛ́*
        even-if    you-are-not(AttrNeg)  there

    (c) *ne*    *ɔ́-kwe-né*         *ɛ́bɛ́ ŋgbɛ*
        but    you-fell(RelPst)    law of-*Ngbɛ*

    (d)             *á-nyɛ́*              *wɔ*
                   they-ate(Pst)        you

2(a) '*Ngbɛ* is an organization (b) which works for the good of the village.

3(a) It has laws (b) which make the village (c) go well.

4(a) Whether you are a member (b) or not, (c) once you break one of the laws of the organization, (d) you are fined'.

In this extract, the relative nonpast is seen in 2(b) as well as in 3(b) and (c). Its function in these instances, as in other parts of the text, is to identify a thing or person and to make a general characterization of him or it. In 2(b), this mode characterizes the organization, *ŋgbɛ*, in contrast with other things. Of course, this contrast is implicit. *Ŋgbɛ*, thus, is identified as an organization that works for the good of the society. This, of course, is the identification of a general condition. Similarly, in 3(b-c), there is the identification of the laws, which exist for the smooth running of the village. In the text quoted earlier (sec. 5.2.1) sentence 4(a) contains the relative nonpast mode in a clause that identifies poverty in contrast with other things.

An example of relative past in the above extract is in 4(c). It too identifies something; however, it is shown not as a general condition but as a specific one, namely, one who has violated the laws of *ŋgbɛ*. The action of violating the laws is a particular action and indicates the man's specific condition.

It may be emphasized here that the use of the relative mode in Dényá, particularly relative past, differs from English or French. Examples 3(c) and 4(c), in English, for example, would not use the relative. Use of the relative in Dényá has to do with staging or the way a speaker controls the perspective from which he presents everything he says.

**5.2.3 The conditional mode.** A quick glance at example 65 (see sec. 5.2.1) shows the conditional mode in sentences 5(a), 7(a), and 8(a), indicating conditions for the following explanations. This function is similar to what is noted in hortatory texts, where the conditional mode is used to state a specific condition for a particular injunction (see 6.2.4 and fig. 19 in sec. 6.3).

**5.3 Summary**

In expository discourse in Dényá, the use of modes depends on whether the proposition is part of the exposition-line or not. Also, stative verb forms have a more prominent place in explanatory texts than in other kinds of text. This is understandable because in descriptions or explanations one usually states what is — not events that have happened. Nonpast is the deep-structure mode for exposition. In other kinds of texts, there may be embedded expository parts. The use of the nonpast in such texts is characteristic. The nonpast encodes general conditions or characteristics, and it also identifies general truths.

The relative nonpast and the relative past modes are also used in expository texts. The relative nonpast mode has the function of identifying a person or thing and characterizing him or it as being in a general condition. The relative past also identifies a person or thing but characterizes him or it as in a specific condition.

The conditional mode is used to state the condition for a specific argument. Its function here is similar to its function in hortatory texts.

# 6 Modes in Hortatory Discourse

When an Anya elder commands or advises a person to perform an activity or to improve his behavior, he uses hortatory discourse. In other words, the purpose of hortatory discourse is to give commands and exhortations. One feature of this discourse genre, unlike others, is the absence of any overt linkage mechanism. It is addressee oriented and is given in the second person.

## 6.1. The Internal Structure of a Hortatory Text

Like texts of other discourse genres, a hortatory text may be divided into introduction, body, and conclusion.

**6.1.1 Introduction.** The introduction may include greetings, injunctions, the topic sentence, the situation, and the purpose of the discourse. The following extract from text E illustrates these:

(67) 1(a) *Negbo,*    *cwɔ́*          *wi*
       Negbo    come(ImpImm)    this-way

    (b)        *jwɔ́lé*        *ka*
            sit(ImpImm)    down

    (c) *m-bɔ́*      *ɛkéké*    *mecɔ́*    *maá-ńjɔɔ́*
       I-took(Pst)    little    speech    to-say

   2(a) *gé*             *wɔ*    *mbɔ*
       see(ImpImm)    you    like-that

    (b) *ɔ́-jyé-ɛ*                 *malɔ*    *bɔɔ́*    *cácá*
       you-who-going(RelNonPst)    towns    people    other

    (c) *muú*    *se*    *wié*    *a-pɔ́*
       person    our    there    he-is-not(AttrNeg)

3   *utɔ́*       *mekálá*       *ne*       *ɔ́-jyé-ɛ-pyɛ́*
    work       white-man       that       you-going-do(RelNonPst)

1(a) 'Negbo, come here, (b) sit down; (c) I have something to tell you.

2(a) There you are, (b) about to leave for foreign lands (c) where none of our people are.

3 It is white man's work you are going to do'.

In this text, there is no greeting. This is due to the nature of the participants involved in the speech act. The speech situation involves a father talking to his son who is about to leave the village for a faraway place to take up his new job. He addresses the son by name, Negbo, and commands him to come. Thus in 1 the speaker-hearer relationship is established. This includes injunctions given in the second person singular.

The topic is announced in 1(c). The speaker announces to the addressee what the discourse is to be about — some advice.

The situation is exemplified in 2(a) to 3. It gives the circumstances that make the discourse necessary. The speaker's intention is to make the listener fully understand his situation and behave in a manner appropriate to it.

**6.1.2 Body.** The body of a hortatory text is very different from the body in other discourse genres. Distinguishing between acts such as preparatory, main, and result on the one hand, and prepeak, peak (climax), and postpeak, on the other, is irrelevant. The body of a hortatory text consists of injunctions (including suggestions) and arguments. In most cases, the two form injunction-argument blocks, with the injunctions forming the exhortation-line, and the arguments the nonexhortations.

The following extract from a text (not included in appendix B) gives an example of an injunction-argument block:

(68) 3(a)       *ɔ-jyɛ-gé*
        (if)    you-went(Cond)

    (b)        *ɔ́-ka-gé*
               you-dare-not(ImpNeg)

    (c)        *ɔ́-nɛ́rɛ́*                         *mekpo    né    metu*
               you-placed(InsistImm)            head     on    play

    (d)        *ɔ́-lí-á*                          *nwɛ     maá-ngí*
               you-left(InsistImm)               book    to-study

    4          *metu    á-cyɛ́ɛ́-gé*                         *muú       geno*
               play    it-gives-not(NonPstNeg)            person     thing

*gefɔ́*
some

5(a)        *ɔ-bɛgé-raŋkáa*                       *nwɛ*
   (if)     you remained know-not(Pst)           book

   (b) *gébé*    *gé-kwɔne-ge*        *nyíɛ*
       time     it-reach(NonPst)     future

   (c) *ɛyigé*   *ɔ-la-li*
       that     you-Hab-cry(Pst)

3(a) 'When you are in school, (b-c) dare not give all your time to playing, (d) forgetting your books.

4 There is no benefit from play.

5(a) If you remained illiterate, (b) there would be a time (c) when you would weep'.

In this extract, sentence 3 contains negative injunctions, or prohibitions. A father is addressing his twelve-year-old son who is about to go to a village school some fifteen kilometers away for the first time. He warns him against certain undesirable actions—a warning encoded with a negative imperative (3b) followed by two insistence forms that in effect make two prohibitions. In sentences 4 and 5 there are arguments to support the injunctions: 4 shows that the addressee will not derive anything from play; 5 shows the painful consequences if the desired course of action is abandoned.

The following is an outline of the rest of the body of this same text:

**INJUNCTION-ARGUMENT BLOCK 2 (7-10)**

Injunction: Don't abandon school.

Argument: The benefits of learning are lasting.

**INJUNCTION-ARGUMENT BLOCK 3 (11-19)**

Injunctions: Be helpful and respectful.

Arguments: That is the behavior expected of a school child. Your teachers are now your parents.

It is important to recognize that injunctions are not all of the same kind. Types of injunctions will be given fuller treatment in the following sections, but it may be worth mentioning here that an injunction can be specific or general, positive or negative. A specific injunction is one expressed with second person (singular or plural) imperative, either positive or negative. A general injunction is inclusive, that is, one that includes the speaker: "Let us do X." An example of a general injunction is found in the same text just quoted in which the father counsels his son to study in school:

(69) 8(a)      *muú*     *a-cyɛé-gé*      *wɔ*   *majyɛé*
     (if)   person   he-gave(Cond)  you  advice

    (b)          *a-ké*
                 he-said(Pst)

    (c)          *líá*          *nwɛ*
                 abandon(ImpImm)  school

    (d)          *cwɔ́*
                 come(ImpImm)

    (e)          *dé-bɛ́*     *fa*
                 we-be(ImpImm)  here

    (f)          *dé-ŋmé-gé*     *gentómé*
                 we-short(ImpAnyt)  hunting

    (g)          *dé-pyɛ́-gé*    *ndé*  *ndé*
                 we-do(ImpAnyt)  what  what

    (h)          *ɔ́-wu-gé*
                 you-listen-not(Imp)

8(a) 'If somebody gives you advice, (b) saying, (c) "Abandon school, (d) come, (e) let us be here, (f) let us be hunting, (g) let us be doing many other things," (h) do not listen to him'.

In this extract, 8(c-g) are general injunctions. They are direct quotations of what the speaker considers to be undesirable courses of action. The *we* does not refer to the speaker of the discourse but to his son's hypothetical distractor. In 8(h), the speaker once more gives a negative injunction in the second person.

**6.1.3 Conclusion.** A conclusion maximally includes a repetition of the topic, final injunctions, and a closure. The following is the conclusion to text E:

(70) 17(a)     *kɛ*          *pere*
             walk(ImpImm)  well

    (b)          *ɔ́-jii-gé*          *nte*
                 you-forget-not(ImpNeg)  thought

    (c) *ɛtíré*  *ń-jɔ-ɔ́*     *mbɔ*
       those   I-said(RelPst)  like-that

    (d)          *jwɔ́-lé*        *cáncá*
              be-staying(ImpAnyt)  well

| (e) | *pyé-gé* | *ńtó* | *utɔ́* | *cáncá* |
|-----|----------|-------|--------|---------|
|     | be-doing(ImpAnyt) | also | work | well |

| (f) *ɛwa* | *é-byé* | *mbɔ* |
|-----------|---------|-------|
| mine | it-finished(Pst) | like-that |

17(a) 'Go well, (b) do not forget (c) what I have said, (d) stay well, (e) be doing your work well; (f) that is all I had to say'.

In 17(c) there is no actual repetition of the topic sentence; instead, the pronoun *etíré* is all that refers to the subject matter of the discourse. The closure comes in 17(f). Injunctions, features of conclusions, are seen in 17(d-e).

## 6.2 The Use of Modes in Hortatory Discourse

In hortatory text, a minumum of some six different types of injunctions occur. For instance, one type requires that the addressee perform the action immediately; others do not require this. Some types are commands. Various verb forms, or modes, are used to encode the different types of injunctions: positive imperative (Imp), negative imperative (ImpNeg), positive exhortation (Hort), past (Pst), and nonpast(NonPst).

The relative modes, both past (RelPst) and nonpast (RelNonPst), and the conditional mode (Cond) do not encode injunctions; they encode other types of discourse information.

### 6.2.1 The imperative modes

**6.2.1.1 The immediate imperative mode.** The immediate imperative mode encodes injunctions that require immediate action on the part of the addressee. This is a feature of introductions of hortatory texts. In text E (see example 63), for example, it is used in the two consecutive injunctions in 1(a) and (b). The verb of such an injunction is in second person singular. This mode may also be used in the body of the text. This is illustrated by example (69), in which 8(c) and (d) are direct quotations and the injunctions are not directed to the hearer. Rather they form part of an imagined situation. Their main function is to make the exhortations more vivid.

In (70), 17(a) is a positive injunction, *kɛ pere* 'Go well'. It expresses the speaker's wish. It also anticipates the closure phrase. The question is whether this injunction can be considered as requiring immediate action. Within the context of this discourse, it could be claimed that this injunction would be followed by an action response from the addressee, for he would soon leave on his journey.

**6.2.1.2 The negative imperative.** The following extract from text E illustrates the use of the negative imperative in hortatory discourse:

(71) 7(a)  *mendé*    *muí*     *ó-ka-gé*
          wife      person    you-dare-not(ImpNeg)

    (b)                        *ó-kwólé*
                              you-follow(InsistImm)

    11     *mendé*    *muí*     *ó-fyɛ-gé*                    *ame*    *wié*
          wife       person    you-put-not(ImpNeg)          eyes     there

    12(a)            *ó-jyé-ɛ*                  *mbɔ*
          (as)      you-going(RelNonPst)       like-that

      (b)            *ó-ka-gé*
                    you-dare-not(ImpNeg)

      (c)            *ó-bá*                     *mendé*    *melɔ*    *cá*
                    you-marry(InsistImm)        wife       village   other

    15     *ó-jii-gé*                          *nte*      *melɔ*
          you-forget-not(ImpNeg)              thought    home

    16(c)  *ó-kɛlé-gé*                         *mejɔó*
          you-seek-not(ImpNeg)                trouble

      (d)  *ó-ŋyu-gé*                          *mmɔó*     *dóó*
          you-drink-not(ImpNeg)               wine       much

7(a) 'Dare not (b) lust after anybody's wife.

11 Do not be attracted to anybody's wife.

12(a) As you are going, (b) dare not (c) marry a foreign woman.

15 Never forget home.

16(c) Don't look for trouble, (d) don't drink a lot'.

A careful study will reveal that 7(a) and (b) constitute a single injunction, as do 12(b) and (c). In each case, the first clause is the negative imperative and the second is the immediate insistence form. Such a combination constitutes the strongest prohibition possible.

**6.2.1.3 The anytime imperative mode.** The anytime imperative mode indicates an exhortation or suggestion, as it was shown in chapter 2. The question to answer now is, What type of injunction does this form encode? The following example from text E is pertinent:

(72) 16(a)           *ɔ-jyɛ-gé*
          (when)    you-go(Cond)

(b) *pyé-gé*                          *utɔɔ́*   *bíɛ*   *cáncá*
be-doing(ImpAnyt)          work       you      well

17(a) *kɛ*                            *pere*
walk(ImpImm)                 well

(b) *ɔ́-jïi-gé*                               *nte*
you-forget-not(ImpNeg)          thought

(c) *ɛtíré*       *ń-jɔ-ɔ́*                   *mbɔ*
which      I-said(RelPst)          like-that

(d) *jwɔ́-lé*                              *cáncá*
be-staying(ImpAnyt)             well

(e) *pyé-gé*                          *ńtó*    *utɔɔ́*   *cáncá*
be-doing(ImpAnyt)          also     work      well

16(a) 'Once there, (b) be doing your work well.

17(a) Go well, (b) don't forget (c) what I have said. (d) Stay well, (e) be doing your work well'.

In 16(b), the speaker exhorts the hearer to be doing his work well. In other words, at any given time, he expects this to be the case. Similarly, in 17(d) and (e), the addressee is asked to keep well and do his work well. These examples show that the anytime imperative mode encodes injunctions to be carried out at any time.

**6.2.2 The nonpast mode.** The function of the nonpast mode in a hortatory text is seen in 73 and 74. Example 73 is from text E, and example 74 is from a text not included in the appendix.

*(73) 4(a)*        *ɔ-jyɛ-gé*
(if)       you-go(Cond)

(b)          *ɔ-pyɛ-ɛ*                     *wiɛ*    *ú-bí*
you-do(NonPst)           same     it

6(a)         *ɔ-jyɛ-gé*                     *éwu*
(if)       you-go(Cond)          there

(b)          *ɔ-gbare-ge*                  *metɔɔ́*   *wíɛ*
you-hold(NonPst)          heart      your

4(a) 'Once there, (b) you should always be doing your work.

6(a) Once there, (b) you should always comport yourself well'.

In both of these exhortations, the addressee is told what he should always be doing. That is the standard expected of him. These injunctions are encoded in the nonpast mode.

(74) 12(a)         *ɔ-ba-gé*              *menɔ*
           (if)    you-marry(Cond)       husband

      (b)          *ɔ-cɛre-ge*            *ji*
                   you-caring-for(NonPst) him

      20(a)        *ɔ-jyɛ-gé*
           (if)    you-go(Cond)

      (b)          *ɔ-noo-ge*             *ji*
                   you-respect(NonPst)    him

      40           *ɔ-pɛ-le*              *menɔ*     *wíɛ*      *cáncá*
                   you-look-after(NonPst) husband    your       well

12(a) 'Once you are married, (b) you should always be taking proper care of him (your husband).

20(a) Once there (in the marital home), (b) you should always respect him.

40 You should always take good care of your husband'.

The three sentences in (74) are part of a hortatory text in which a father advises a daughter he has recently given in marriage. These are some of the things she should always do. She should always take good care of him; she should always respect him. The reason for this is that, if she does this, the husband will also respect her. In 40, she is once more reminded to always take good care of her husband.

The nonpast mode in a hortatory text is seen to encode injunctions that say, "You should always do X." In other words, the injunction requires that the addressee should be in the habit of always doing X—that should constitute his general attitude.

At this point, it might be asked whether there is any semantic difference between injunctions encoded by the anytime imperative, which requires that the addressee do X at any time, and those encoded by the nonpast, which demands that he always do X. Yes, there definitely is a semantic difference between these two types of injunctions. In anytime injunctions, the emphasis is on individual isolated events. In contrast, in the do-it-always injunctions, the focus is not on individual events or actions, but rather on continuous behavior or attitude.

**6.2.3 The past mode.** The past mode, it will be remembered, is the natural mode for events in narrative texts and for preparatory actions in procedural texts. The past mode is also found in hortatory text where it occurs in injunctions that require the addressee to perform some action occasionally. Example 75 is from text E:

(75) 14(a)          ɔ-bɛlé-gé              kpaá
          when      you-slept(Cond)       long

    (b)             ɔ̆-cwɔ́
                    you-came(Pst)

    (c)             ɔ̆-pɛ                  ɛsé
                    you-looked(Pst)       us

14(a) 'After some time, (b) you should come and (c) visit us'.

In example 75, the speaker makes an invitation to the addressee to take some future action. He is expected, after being away for some time, to come visit the speaker (the parents). The action expected is not to be frequent but occasional. These occasional actions are in 14(b) and (c) and are encoded in the past mode. Consider also examples 76-78, which are from text L, also not included in the appendix:

(76) 11(a) jyɛ́ɛ ndé  dondo       ɔ̆-ké
          every      morning      you-said(Pst)

    (b)                           ɔ-jyɛ-ɛ                nnyi
                                  you-going(NonPst)      stream

    (c)                           ɔ̆-kpa                 ŋkwɔ
                                  you-carried(Pst)       pot

(a) 'Whenever you decide (b) to go to the stream, (c) carry a water pot'.

(77) 13(a)       muú      a-tɔ-gé            wɔ     melu
          (if)   person   he-sent(Cond)      you    place

    (b)          ɔ̆-ɍɛ̆
                 you-went(Pst)

(a) 'If you are sent on any errand, (b) you should go'.

(78) 15(a)          ɔ-sɛ-gé               holide
          (when)    you-received(Cond)    holiday

    (b)             ɔ-cwɔ́
                    you-come(Pst)

    (c)             ɔ-gé ɛsé
                    you-saw(Pst) us

(a) 'When you holiday, come and see us'.

Each past mode in these examples indicates what should be done occasionally. In 77, for example, the speaker exhorts the addressee to give help when somebody requires him to do so. It is to be expected that such help will be demanded only occasionally. In 78, the hearer is expected to come home occasionally, when he has holidays.

**6.2.4 The use of modes in nonexhortatory propositions.** As mentioned earlier, in nonexhortatory clauses the mode does not determine an injunction. This is seen in the following examples from text E (only predicates are indicated):

(79) 2(b) *ɔ́-jyɛ́-ɛ* '*you who are going*'
        (RelNonPst): identification/description of listener

   2(c) *a-pɔ́* '*he is not*'
        (AttrNeg): specific condition

   3    *ɔ́-jyɛ́-ɛ-pyɛ́* '*you who are going to do*'
        (RelNonPst): same as 2(b)

   4(a) *ɔ-jyɛ-gé* '*if you go*'
        (Cond): condition for a specific injunction

   5(a) *á-ku-ú* '*he called*'
        (RelPst): same as 2(b)

   6(a) *ɔ-jyɛ-gé* '*if you go*'
        (Cond): same as 4(a)

   8(a) *a-lu* '*she is*'
        (Attr): identification used as argument

   9(a) *a-lu* '*she is*'
        (Attr): same as 8(a)

  10(b) *á-gbɔ́* '*they died*'
        (Pst): identification as a resulting condition

  12(d) *ɔ-ba-gé* '*if you marry*'
        (Cond): same as 4(a)

  12(e) *ɔ́-la* '*you remained*'
        (Pst): same as 10(b)

  14(a) *ɔ-bɛlé-gé* '*if you sleep*'
        (Cond): same as 4(a)

  16(a) *ɔ-jyɛ-gé* '*if you go*'
        (Cond): same as 4(a)

Nonexhortatory predicates are of two kinds: those that contain a verb inflected for mode and those that do not. The former are predicates with event verbs and the latter are nominal predicates.

Now concerning event predicates, some comments are added relative to those predicates that contain the conditional and relative modes. The conditional mode, as shown by the examples above as well as by other texts, gives the condition for a specific injunction. In most of the examples quoted throughout this chapter, the conditional mode precedes the mode determining the injunction. In example 78, for instance, 15(a) is a specific condition for the injunctions in 15(b) and (c): (a) 'When you have a holiday, (b) come and (c) visit us'. This use of the conditional mode in hortatory discourse, it should be noted, differs from its use in narrative and procedural.

The relative modes, past and nonpast, are also used to state conditions. The relative nonpast states a general condition or characteristic. This is exemplified by 2(b) and 3 in example 79. The relative past states a specific condition or characteristic; 5(a) is an example of this use.

### 6.3 Hierarchy of the injunctions

This chapter has shown that in hortatory texts, injunctions may be found in the introduction, body, and conclusion. It has also been made evident that the injunctions are of different kinds. What needs to be attempted now is to place these injunctions in some kind of hierarchy.

Injunctions, as has been shown, are action response utterances. An injunction requiring immediate action should be ranked higher on the scale of action response than one that demands delayed action. One that says, "You should always" ought to be higher than one that says, "You should occasionally."

In view of this, the injunctions that have been discussed can be ranked on a descending order as shown in figure 18.

| TYPE OF INJUNCTION | | MODE |
|---|---|---|
| Immediate | | Immediate Imperative |
| Anytime | Positive (do) | Anytime Imperative |
| | Negative (don't) | Negative Imperative |
| Always | (You should) | Nonpast |
| Occasionally | (You should sometimes) | Past |

Fig. 18. Hierarchy of the injunctions

The information given in figure 18 can be represented equally well by a tree diagram. Figure 19 summarizes the relationships between modes and injunctions. It also shows that the conditional, the relative past, and the relative nonpast modes are not used to encode injunctions. The conditional mode specifies the condition governing an injunction. The relative past and the relative nonpast modes identify by characterization the addressee or the thing being talked about.

The mode for immediate injunctions is the immediate imperative, while the mode for anytime prohibitions is the negative imperative. The anytime imperative encodes do-it-anytime injunctions. The mode for injunctions requiring occasional (sometimes) actions by the addressee is the past. The nonpast mode encodes do-it-always injunctions.

Thus, it is clear that the choice of one mode in preference to another is not haphazard. There are definite semantic correlations involved.

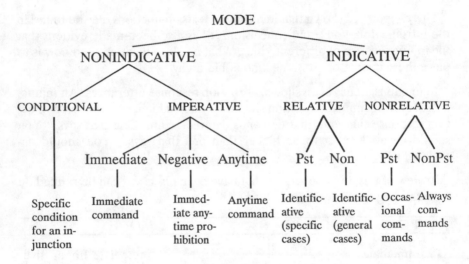

Fig. 19. Tree diagram of the relationships between modes and injunctions

# 7 Conclusion

The purpose of this study has been to account for the use of Dényá verb forms in connected discourse. It is a study in discourse analysis, or what is now commonly known as text linguistics.

It has been shown that Dényá is not a language with heavy affixation. The verb forms are a combination of tone and certain affixes. After the consideration of matters such as phonology, noun classes, and order typology in chapter 1, in chapter 2 the different kinds of verb forms and their relationships with each other are described.

The main study has been of the use of modes (verb forms) in various types of discourse. Text linguists are more and more aware that mere descriptive statements about grammatical categories are not enough: "It is one thing to describe the internal structure of a verb in a language with heavy affixation. It is something else to know where to use one verb form rather than another" (Longacre 1977:72).

Two aspects of the use of modes in Dényá discourse have become evident. First, some verb forms are associated with different discourse genres. The occurrence of a certain verb form immediately suggests the discourse type. Figure 20 shows the relationship between modes and discourse genres.

| Genre (Discourse Type) | Mode |
|---|---|
| Narrative | Past |
| Procedural | Past |
| Expository | Nonpast |
| Hortatory | Imperative/Past/Nonpast |

Fig. 20. Correlation between discourse type and mode

85

Second, this study has revealed that one cannot use with real assurance any mode (verb form) in Dényá without a knowledge of its discourse structure. Discourse structure has been described in terms of discourse information. Events, for example, in narrative discourse are not all of the same importance. The most important events are the climactic ones. Climactic events are often differentiated from nonclimactic by change of mode. There are different kinds of nonevents also in narrative discourse.

In other discourse types, discourse information is given in terms of procedures and nonprocedures, explanations and nonexplanations, and exhortations and nonexhortations. Within each discourse type, various subtypes have been established.

In each type of text there are preferred verb forms that tend to advance the discourse and others which mark material that is of secondary importance. Figure 21 is a summary of the use of modes as discussed in chapters 3-6.

| MODE | USE IN DISCOURSE |
|------|------------------|
| 1. Past | (a) Basic mode for event-line in narrative texts and for procedure-line in procedural texts; statistically most frequent; its main function is to advance the event-line or procedure-line |
| | (b) Marks preparatory or nonclimactic events or actions in narrative and procedural discourses |
| | (c) If used to state the moral of a story, it indicates the conclusion drawn |
| | (d) Encodes do-it-occasionally injunctions in hortatory discourse |
| 2. Nonpast | (a) Gives further information about a character already introduced in a stative clause, characterizing him in terms of his activities or an existing relationship |
| | (b) Links the major parts of a narrative text |
| | (c) Marks climactic events or main actions within an episode of either a narrative or a procedural text |
| | (d) Identifies the main event of two concurrent ones |
| | (e) Marks material as background in narrative and procedural discourse |
| | (f) Identifies general conditions, characteristics, or truths in expository discourse |

| MODE | USE IN DISCOURSE |
|---|---|
|  | (g) Encodes do-it-always injunctions in hortatory discourse |
| 3. Conditional | (a) Provides the linkage mechanism in a procedural text; marks completed actions |
|  | (b) States specific condition for an injunction in a hortatory text and for an explanation in an explanatory text |
| 4. Relative nonpast | (a) Further identifies participants |
|  | (b) Characterizes a participant, an event, or an action as a general condition |
| 5. Relative past | (a) Further identifies participants. |
|  | (b) Characterizes an event or action as a specific circumstance or condition |
| 6. Repetitive aspect | Contributes to cohesion of a discourse as an anaphoric marker, the repeated action referring back to an earlier action |
| 7. Inceptive aspect | Marks the focal point, or climax, of a set of actions in narrative or procedural discourse |
| 8. Habitual aspect | (a) Marks the results of events and occurs at the conclusion of a narrative |
|  | (b) Marks what happens to the end product in a procedural text |
| 9. Immediate imperative | (a) Encodes immediate injunctions |
|  | (b) Indicates the end of the speaker-hearer dimension in the introduction of a narrative discourse and acts as a link to the stage |
|  | (c) Indicates the speaker-hearer relationship in the conclusion of a narrative |
| 10. Anytime imperative | (a) Encodes injunctions to be carried out any time |
| 11. Negative imperative | Encodes immediate or anytime prohibitions |

Fig. 21. Summary of the use of mode in the four discourse genres

It has been shown that the discourse genres posited by Longacre are basic to Dényá discourse and that Grimes's categories of discourse information, though originally applied to the narrative, are nonetheless invaluable ingredients of these genres.

If the goal of discourse analysis is to study the production of new meaning in texts (Wienold 1978:133), there is no doubt that this study has reached that goal. It has established new meanings of the verb forms in Dényá discourse.

# Appendix A: Phonology, Noun Classes, Order Typology

No linguistic description of Dényá exists. For that reason a brief account of the Dényá sound system is now given. The noun class system, common to all Bantu languages, is also described briefly, and some notes on the basic order typology are given.

**1 Phonology**

| Place of Articulation | | LABIALS | ALVEOLAR | PALATAL | VELAR | LABIO-VELAR |
|---|---|---|---|---|---|---|
| Manner of Articulation | | | | | | |
| PLOSIVES | vl | p | t | c | k | kp |
|  | vd | b | d | j | g | gb |
| FRICATIVES | vl | f | s | sh | | |
|  | vd | v | | | | |
| NASALS | | m | n | ny | ŋ | ŋm |
| VIBRANT/ FLAP | | | r | | | |
| CONTINUANTS | | w | l | y | | |

Fig. 22. Dényá consonants

All consonant phonemes, except *r*, *w*, and *y*, contrast with their labialized and palatalized counterparts, which are considered to be unit phonemes. Labialized consonants are written *Cw*, and palatalized consonants are written *Cy*. Consonants occur only syllable initially.

|        | FRONT | CENTRAL | BACK |
|--------|-------|---------|------|
| HIGH   | i     |         | u    |
| MID    | e     |         | o    |
| LOW    | ɛ     | a       | ɔ    |
| NASAL  | N     |         |      |

Fig. 23. Dényá vowels

Any vowel may be repeated, making a sequence of two vowels of the same quality. Thus, for example, /i/ and /ii/ are contrastive, and if such a sequence occurred as syllable peak, the result would be interpreted as two syllables, CV and V. The vowels may occur with or without tone glides, as the following show:

| (a) *a-jyɛɛ* | 'he is going' |
| (b) *a-cyɛɛ́* | 'he gave' |

| (a) *mboó* | 'short' |
| (b) *a-boo* | 'he is running' |

Tone is significant in syllables, including syllabic nasals. There are two tones: high and low. High is marked (´); low is unmarked. The following are contrastive pairs:

| (a) *tí* | 'pierce' |
| (b) *ti* | 'wipe' |

| (a) *bé* | 'dance' |
| (b) *be* | 'war' |

| (a) *bá* | 'marry' |
| (b) *ba* | 'stick on' |

| (a) *a-fé* | 'he went' |
| (b) *á-fé* | 'they went' |

| (a) *a-wane* | 'he is killing' |
| (b) *á-wáne* | 'he who is killing' |
| (c) *á-wané* | 'he who killed' |

| CLASS | PROTO-BANTU FORM | NOUN PREFIX | EXAMPLES | |
|---|---|---|---|---|
| 1 | sg. *mo* | *n-, me* *m-* | *muú* *nnté* *mfwa* | 'person' 'father' 'chief' |
| 2 | pl. *va-* | *a-, b-* | *bɔɔ́* *anté* *afwa* | 'persons/people' 'fathers' 'chiefs' |
| 3 | sg. *mo-* | *ɛ-* | *ɛ-saá* *ɛkwíá* *ɛ-tɛ* | 'cutlass' 'wooden ladle' 'duiker' |
| 4 | pl. *me* | *de-* | *desaá* *dekwíá* *detɛ* | 'cutlasses' 'wooden ladles' 'duikers' |
| 5 | sg. *le* | *me-* | *mekpɔ* *mektɔɔ́* *mekwa* | 'head' 'heart' 'box' |
| 6a | pl. *ma* | *ma-* | *makpo* *maktɔɔ́* *makwa* | 'heads' 'hearts' 'box' |
| 6b | *ma* | *ma- m-* *n-* | *manaá* *mmɔɔ́* *njegése* | 'water' 'wine' 'ground nuts' |
| 7 | sg. *ke-* | *ge-* | *géba* *gepú* *gepa* | 'bag' 'house' 'wound' |
| 8 | pl. *vi* | *u-* | *úba* *upú* *upa* | 'bags' 'houses' 'wounds' |
| 9 | sg. ne | *N-* | *ŋmŋme* *mpɔ* *meshu* | 'goat' 'cow' 'elephant' |
| 10 | pl. | | *ŋmŋme* *mpɔ* *meshu* | 'goats' 'cows' 'elephants' |

Fig. 24. Dényá noun classes

Tone glides are analysed as sequences of two tones, but $\check{V}$ is used instead of $V\acute{V}$ to mark tone glides on lengthened vowels. There is also downstepping of high tones; this is not marked differently from high tone.

The evidence for this phonological analysis will be published elsewhere. As far as the data here are concerned, the standardization process has not yet begun; therefore, certain inconsistencies may be observed.

## 2. Noun Classes

Dényá is a noun class language. It has been possible to establish eleven noun classes. In figure 24 these are numbered to correspond to the Proto-Bantu (PB) noun classes. The PB prefixes used are taken from Welmers (1973:165).

The classes may be grouped in pairs, called genders, which represent singular and plural contrasts. There are the following two-class genders: 1/2, 3/4, 3/6a, 5/6a, 7/8, 8/6a, 9/10. In addition, there are these one-class genders: 4, 6b, and 8.

The noun classes are shown in figure 24.

## 3 Basic Order Typology

Greenberg (1963) distinguished three types of languages on the basis of their sentence constituents. Though Heine (1976) criticized this classification as being overly idealized, it remains the most widely accepted. In type 1 languages, the verb comes before the subject and the object, VSO. In type 2, the verb comes between the subject and object, SVO; and in type 3 both subject and object precede the verb, SOV.

According to this classification, Dényá is a type 2 language, i.e., SVO, like most Benue-Congo languages including Bantu. The genetive, the possessive adjective, and the descriptive adjective follow the noun in Dényá. Prepositions occur in Dényá, as in other SVO languages.

# Appendix B: Texts

Text A Why an Elephant Always Dies Near a Stream

Text B How Ŋkpɛɛ́ Prevented His Divorce

Text C How to Make a Sleeping Mat

Text D Ngbɛ Society

Text E Always Do Your work Well

**TEXT A: Why an Elephant Always Dies Near a Stream**

| Nar: 1 | *ɛkame* | | *yɔɔ* | | |
| | story | | [call for audience response] | | |
| Aud: 2 | | | *yɔɔ* | | |
| | | | [response] | | |
| Nar: 3(a) | | | *gé-ó* | | |
| | | | hear(ImpImm) | | |
| (b) | *gébé* | *gefɔ́* | *gébɔ́* | *gé-lú* | |
| | time | Indef | it | was (Attr) | |
| (c) | *ɛyígé* | *meshu* | *á-nɛ-né* | | *ɛpaá* |
| | when | Elephant | he-(who)-invited(RelPst) | | feast |
| 4(a) | | | *a-ké* | | |
| | | | he-said(Pst) | | |
| (b) | | | *á-jyɛ́* | | |
| | | | they-go(ImpImm) | | |
| (c) | | | *á-tɔ́* | *mekɔɔ́* | *wuí* |
| | | | they-clear(ImpImm) | farm | for-him |
| 5(a) | | | *á-fɛ́* | | |
| | | | they-went(Pst) | | |

93

(b)                          á-tó                mekɔɔ́ ntó   nemeé
                             they-cleared(Pst)  farm   also  much

(c)      mekɔɔ́              é-ŋeá
         farm               it-big(Attr)

6(a) ne                     á-tané
     and                    they-left(Pst)

(b)                         á-wilé               mmu
                            they-returned(Pst)   home

7(a)     meshu              a-tyɛɛ́ menyɛɛ́
         Elephant           he-prepared(Pst) food

(b)                         a-cyɛɛ́
                            he-gave(Pst)

(c)                         a-ké
                            he-said(Pst)

(d)                         á-nyɛ́
                            they-eat(ImpImm)

8                           ányɛ́        menyɛɛ́ ká    káká
                            they-ate(Pst) food   for   long

9(a)                        a-karé               menyɛɛ́
                            he-divided(Pst)      food

(b)                         ǎ-cyɛ́ɛ́-fɔ́                     negiá  wɔ́
                            he-gave-really not(PstNeg)    Crab   neg

10   negiá                  a-lu         mbɔ      maá    nnyi
     Crab                   he-was Attr  certainly child  stream

11(a) ne        negiá       a-jyɛ-fyɛ́            ula     ne    muú
      however   Crab        he-went-put(Pst)     bottom  with  person

(b)     yi                  á-tyɛ́ɛ-ge                  menyɛɛ́
        who                 he-cooks(RelNonPst)        food

(c)                         á-cyɛ́ɛ-ge                      meshu
                            he-gives(RelNonPst)    (to)    Elephant

12(a)                       a-ké
                            he-said(Pst)

(b)                         á-fyɛ́                ŋkale   dɔɔ́
                            he-put(ImpImm)       pepper  much

13(a)    átá    meshu       a-tɔ́           ɛtɛ
         Papa   Elephant    he-sent(Pst)   Duiker

(b) ńnó  a-jyɛ-cwɛ́               manaá  né    maá   nnyi
    so-that he-went-fetched(Pst) water  from  child stream

14     *ɛtɛ*          *af-é*
         Duiker       he-went(Pst)

15(a)               *a-kwɔné*       *maá*   *nnyi*
                      he-arrived(Pst)  child  stream

  (b)               *a-jya*          *ntaá*
                      he-stepped-on(Pst)  stone

16(a)  *negiá*       *a-gií*
         Crab         he-asked(Pst)

  (b)               *a-ké*
                      he-said(Pst)

  (c) *ndé*  *mú*    *á-jya-lé*                 *ntaá*   *ninembɔ*
     what  person  he-who-stepped-on(RelPst)  stone  that

17(a)   *ɛtɛ*          *a-ké*
        Duiker       he-said (Pst)

  (b)               *lé*        *me*  *ɛtɛ*
                      it-is(Attr)  I  Duiker

  (c) *ne*   *ń-jya-lé*         *mbɔ*  *ntaá*   *ninembɔ*
     who  I-stepped(RelPst)  like  stone  that

18(a) *negiá*        *a-gií*       *ji*
     Crab         he-asked(Pst)  him

  (b)               *a-ké*
                      he-said(Pst)

  (c)               *ɔ́-cwɔ-pyɛ́*        *ndé*
                    you-came-make(Pst)  what

19(a)   *ɛtɛ*        *a-ké*
        Duiker       he-said(Pst)

  (b)               *ň-cwɔ-tú*       *manaá*
                    I-came-fetch(Pst)  water

  (c)               *ň-jyɛ-cyɛ́*     *átá*  *meshu*
                    I-went-give(Pst)  Papa  Elephant

20(a) *negiá*        *a-ké*       *ne*  *ji*
     Crab         he-said(Pst)  to  him

  (b) *átá*  *meshu*  *yi*  *á-nyɛ-ɛ́*    *menyɛɛ́*
     Papa  Elephant  who  he-ate(RelPst)  food

  (c)               *á-nyo-mé*         *me?*
                  he-(who)-refused(RelPst)  me

  (d) *ne*           *ɔ́-cwɔ-tú*          *manaá*
     and       you-(who)-came-fetch(RelPst)  water

(e)                          *ɔ́-jyé-ɛ-cyéɛ*                    *ji*
                             you-go-give(RelNonPst)   him

21(a) *manaá    mimbɔ    má-pɔ́*
      water       that       it-not(AttrNeg)

   (b)                       *có-gáré*                     *ji*
                             go-tell(ImpImm)         him

22(a) *ɛtɛ      a-keré            meso*
      Duiker   he-turned(Pst)   back

   (b)                       *a-cwɔ-gáre*               *meshu*
                             he-came-told(Pst)   Elephant

   (c)                       *a-ké*
                             he-said(Pst)

   (d) *negiá*               *a-gbɛ́*                    *manaá*
       Crab                  he-shut-off(Pst)   water

   (e)                       *a-ké*
                             he-said

   (f)                       *ń-cwɔ-gé*
                             I-come-fetch-not(ImpNeg)

23(a) *meshu    metɔ́ɔ    ɛ́-sɔ́*             *ji*
      Elephant   heart    it-hot(Pst)     him

   (b)                       *a-la-kulé*               *ne    gelu    geŋkale*
                             he-Hab-left(Pst)   with   power  of pepper

   (c) *yí      gé-lú*                    *mbɔ      ji    metɔ́ɔ*
       which   it-is(RelNonPst)   like-that   him   heart

24(a) *gátɛlé    gátɛlé    a-kwɔ́*              *né   maá    nnyi*
      running   running   he-arrived(Pst)   at    child   stream

   (b) *ńnó      ji*        *a-jyé*
       so-that   him        he-went(Pst)

   (c)                       *a-gií*                    *negiá*
                             he-asked(Pst)   Crab

   (d) *ńnó      ndé*        *gé-pyɛ-gé*
       how      what         it-happened(RelPst)

   (e) *ne*                   *ɔ́-gbɛ-ɛ́*                 *manaá?*
       that                  you-shut-off(RelPst)   water

25(a)                        *a-kwé*
                             he-fell(Pst)

   (b)                       *a-gbó*                    *ɛfi*
                             he-died(Pst)   there

|            | *mbale* | *maá* | *nnyi* |
|---|---|---|---|
|            | side    | child | stream |

26(a)     *gé*                    *ŋkaá*      *wú*
          see(ImpImm)            reason      why

(b) *ne jyɛɛ́*     *ɔ́-ŋmé*          *meshu*      *ɛ́fɔ́*
    even if        you-shot(Pst)    elephant    where

(c)       *a-jyɛ-ɛ*                *wié*  *mbaá*
          he-goes(NonPst)          just   where

(d) *maá   nnyi*     *a-lú*
    child  stream    it-is(Attr)

(e) *ne*            *a-la-gbɔ́*
    before          it-Hab-died(Pst)

27(a)     *á-ké*
          they-said(Pst)

(b)       *á-kwɔ-ɔ*                    *meshu*
          they-butcher(NonPst)         elephant

(c)       *á-nyu-u*                   *manaá*
          they-drink(NonPst)          water

**Free translation of text A**

1. Listen to a story! 2. We listen. 3. (a) Hear, (b) there was a time (c) when Elephant invited people to a feast. 4. (a) He asked people (b) to go and (c) clear his farm. 5. (a) They went (b) and did clear a big farm. (c) The farm was really big. 6. (a) Then, they left (the farm) and (b) returned home. 7. (a) Elephant prepared food. (b) He gave it (to people) and (c) asked (d) them to eat. 8. They ate a lot of food. 9. (a) Elephant shared the food, (but) (b) he did not give any to Crab. 10. Crab was then in a small stream. 11. (a) However, Crab went and connived with the man (b) who cooks food and (c) serves it to Elephant. 12. (a) Crab told him (b) to put a lot of pepper (in the food). 13. (a) (Having eaten,) Papa Elephant sent Duiker (b) to go and fetch water from the stream. 14. Duiker went. 15. (a) He reached the stream and (b) stepped on a stone. 16. (a) Crab asked — (b) he demanded — (c) "Who is the person who stepped on that stone?" 17. (a) Duiker said, (b) "I, Duiker, (c) stepped on that stone." 18. (a) Crab asked him, (b) he said, (c) "What have you come for?" 19. (a) Duiker said, (b) "I have come to fetch water (c) for Papa Elephant." 20. (a) Crab said, (b) "Is it Papa Elephant who ate food (c) and refused to give me some? (d) You have come to carry water (e) to go and give him? 21. (a) There is no water for him, (b) go and tell him." 22. (a) Duiker returned. (b) He came and told Elephant, (c) he said, (d) "Crab shut off the water. (e) He ordered me

(f) not to fetch any." 23. (a) Elephant was angry, (b) with the pepper (c) still paining him. 24. (a) With a non-stop run, he arrived at the small stream (b) to go (c) and ask Crab, (d) "Why (e) did you shut off the water?" 25. (a) At that moment he fell, (b) and died there at the bank of the small stream. 26. (a) That is why, (b) even if you shoot an elephant anywhere, (c) it always goes (d) to where there is a stream (e) before it dies. 27. (a) As a result, (b) when it is being butchered, (c) people can also drink water.

### DENYA  TEXT B: How Ŋkpɛɛ́ Prevented His Divorce

| Nar: 1 | | | ɛkame<br>story | yɔɔ<br>[call for audience response] | | |
|---|---|---|---|---|---|---|
| Aud: 2 | | | | yɔɔ<br>[response] | | |
| 3(a) | | | | gé-ó<br>see(ImpImm) | | |
| (b) | ŋkpɛɛ́<br>Ŋkpɛɛ́ | ne<br>and | | á-lú<br>he-who-is(RelNonPst) | | |
| (c) | | | | a-bɔ́<br>he-took(Pst) | | |
| (d) | | | | a-pɔ́<br>he-is-not(AttrNeg) | ne<br>with | mendé<br>wife |
| 4(a) ne<br>and | újiá<br>morning | a-jyɛ-bá<br>he-went-married(Pst) | | | mendé<br>wife | wuú<br>his |
| (b) | | | | a-cwɔ́<br>he-came(Pst) | | |
| 5(a) ɛbwɔ́ ne ji<br>them | | | | á-bɛle-ge<br>they-sleep(NonPst) | | |
| (b) | | | | á-bɛle-ge<br>they-sleep(NonPst) | | |
| (c) | | | | á-bɛle-ge<br>they-sleep(NonPst) | | |
| 6 újiá a-cwɔ-fyɛ́ mendé wuú mabɛ́<br>morning he-came-put(Pst) wife his laws | | | | | | |
| 7(a) | | | | a-ké<br>he-said(Pst) | | |

(b) *émâ*              *m-bɛlé-gé*      *géjá*   *ne*   *maa*
    one               I-slept(Cond)   sleep   in    child

                        *gepú*   *wa*
                        house   my

(c)              *ɔ̌-ké*
          you-said(Pst)

(d)              *ɔ-kpɛ-ne*              *wié*
         you-enter(NonPst)   there

(e)              *do*              *menómbɪ*
         knock(ImpImm)   door

8    *pɔ*              *ɔ̌-wú*
   [excl]            you-heard(Pst)

9          *mendé*      *a-kamé*
      wife         she-agreed(Pst)

10(a)         *a-ma-fyɛ́*      *ɛwí*     *fɔ*
        he-Rep-put(Pst)   another   one

(b)            *a-ké*
      he-said(Pst)

(c) *jyɛɛ́*   *ne*   *utuúí*   *ne*     *ŋ̌-ké*
   even    at    night   that   I-said(Pst)

(d)            *m-bɛle-ge*
      I-sleep(NonPst)

(e)            *ɔ̌-ké*
      you-said(Pst)

(f)            *ɔ-cwɔ-ɔ-kpɛ́*            *maá*   *gepú*   *wa*
      you-coming(NonPst)   child   house   my

(g)            *ɔ́-lwɛ-gé*            *mewɛ*
      you-light-not(ImpNeg)   light

(h) *ɔ̌-cwɔ́*          *ne*    *ɛwú*
   you-came(Pst)   with   it

11         *pɔ́,*              *ɔ̌-wú*
      [excl]            you-heard(Pst)

12         *mendé*      *a-kamé*
      wife         she-accepted(Pst)

13(a) *újiá*      *bií*   *fɔ́,*   *ŋkpɛɛ́*   *a-jyɛ-nyú*         *mmɔɔ́*
     morning   day,   indef   Ŋkpɛɛ́   he-went-drank(Pst)   wine

(b)            *má-pyɛ*         *ji*
      it-caught(Pst)   him

(c)                                  *a-kwé*        *géjá*
                                     he-fell(Pst)   asleep

(d)                                  *a-lá-béle*
                                     he-Incep-slept(Pst)

(e)          *ndeé*                  *é-fo*         *ula*
             cloth                   it-left(Pst)   buttocks

14(a)        *ŋkpɛέ*                 *a-lu*              *ula*        *cuu*
             Ŋkp-ɛέ                  he-has(Attr)       buttocks     red

(b) *mabέ*   *yí*    *ji*    *á-fyé-ɛ*                   *mbɔ*
    laws     which   her     he-gives(RelNonPst)         like-that

(c)                                  *a-bi-i*
                                     he-conceals(NonPst)

(d) *ńnó*                            *é-ka-gé*
    so that                          it-known-not(ImpNeg)

(e)          *mendé*                 *a-gέ*
             wife                    she-saw(Pst)

(f) *ŋkane*  *ula*                   *ú-gɛlé*                    *ji*
    as       buttocks               they-became-red(Attr)       him

15(a) *ne*   *bií*  *bí*  *mbɔ*  *mendé*  *a-jií*                *nte*
      but    day    that-one   wife    she-forgot(Pst)          thought

(b)                                  *a-ké*
                                     she-said(Pst)

(c)                                  *a-kpɛ-ne*                 *ne*   *uluí*
                                     she-enters(NonPst)        at     night

(d)                                  *a-kpá*             *mewɛ*
                                     she-carried(Pst)    light

16(a)                                *a-ké*
                                     she-said(Pst)

(b)                                  *a-jyɛ-ɛ*
                                     she-goes(NonPst)

(c) *ŋkpɛέ*    *a-pɔ́-sê*                         *ne*   *ndeé*  *ula*
    Ŋkpɛέ      he-had-no-longer(PstNeg)          with   cloth   buttocks

17(a)                                *a-gέ*
                                     she-saw(Pst)

(b) *ŋkane*   *ula*                  *ú-gɛlé*            *ji,*   *ŋkpɛέ*
    as        buttocks              they-red(Attr)      him     Ŋkpɛέ

18(a)        *ayi*   *mendé*  *a-cwa*                   *ɛlúlí*
             the     wife     she-shouted(Pst)          [shout]

(b) *saá    njí    menɔ    wa    yi    ḿ-bané*
    so     indeed  husband  my    that   I-married(RelPst)

*na*
from-beginning

(c)                          *a-lu        ula      cuu*
                             he-is(Attr)  buttocks  red

(d) *esé    ne    ji    n-lia-ge          ji*
    we     and   he    I-leave(NonPst)    him

19                           *a-jyɛ-béle*
                             she-went-slept(Pst)

20(a) *újíágé    a-la                      geféré    geféré*
      morning   she-remained(Pst)         moody     moody

(b) *menɔ      wuú    a-gií             ji*
    husband    her    he-asked(Pst)     her

(c)                          *a-ké*
                             he-said

(d) *mmá,    ndé    mecɔ?*
    madam   what    thing

21(a)                        *a-ké*
                             she-said(Pst)

(b) *saá    njí ɔ-lu        na                   ula       cuu*
    so     you-are(Attr)   from-the-beginning   buttocks  red

(c)            *ne    ɔ́-bí-i                      me*
               that   you-conceal(RelNonPst)      mc

(d) *ńnuí                    ɔ-kame gɛ̀*
    so-that                  you-allow-not(ImpNeg)

(e)            *me          ŋ̌-kaá*
               I            I-knew(Pst)

22(a)          *ne    njuí         ŋ̌-kaá         yɛ́*
               but    yesterday    I-knew(Pst)   then

(b) *ne    esé    ne    wɔ    neba        né-byɛ́*
    and   our    and   your   marriage    it-finished(Pst)

(c)            *me          n-jyɛ-ɛ*
               I            I-go(NonPst)

23(a)          *ŋkpɛɛ́    a-kwɔ            mata*
               Ŋkpɛɛ́     he-begged(Pst)   jaws

(b)                          *a-cyɛɛ́         unó*
                             he-gave(Pst)    things

(c)                              *a-cyɛɛ́*              *ŋka*
                                 he-gave(Pst)        money

(d)                              *a-cyɛɛ́*              *menya*
                                 he-gave(Pst)        meat

24(a)        *mendé*              *a-sɛ́*
             wife                she-received(Pst)

(b)                              *a-gɔ́*
                                 she-allowed(Pst)

25(a)    *jyɛɛ́*    *ndé*    *bí*    *ne*    *á-kwé*          *ɛkɛ́kɛ́*   *mawané*
         every   what   day    and   they-fell(Pst)   little    quarrel

(b)          *mendé*              *a-kɛ́*
             wife                she-said(Pst)

(c)                              *a-jyɛ-ɛ*
                                 she-goes(NonPst)

(d) *mbaá*   *ndéne*   *ji*    *a-cwɔ-ɔ-bá*                        *menɔ*
     why     that    her    she-come-marries(NonPst)      husband

(e)          *yi*    *á-lú*                    *ula*        *cuu*
             who    he-is(RelNonPst)   buttocks    red

26(a)                            *a-kɛ́*
                                 she-said(Pst)

(b)                              *a-jyɛ-ɛ*                    *ji*
                                 she-goes(NonPst)        her

27(a)        *ŋkpɛɛ́*              *a-kwɔ́*             *mata*
             Ŋkpɛɛ́               he-begged(Pst)     jaws

(b)                              *a-cyɛɛ́*              *unó*    *wié*    *mbɔ*
                                 he-gave(Pst)        thing   there   like-that

28(a)                            *kwɔ-ɔ*
                                 begging(NonPst)

(b)                              *kwɔ-ɔ*
                                 begging(NonPst)

(c)                              *kwɔ-ɔ*
                                 begging(NonPst)

(d)          *ji*    *nto*    *a-pwa*
             him    also    he-tired(Pst)

29(a)    *ujiá*              *á-ma-kwé*              *ma wá mé*
         morning           they-Rep-fell(Pst)     quarrel

(b)          *mendé*              *a-kɛ́*
             wife                she-said(Pst)

(c)       *a-jyɛɛ*
         she-going(NonPst)

30(a)  *ŋkpɛɛ́*   *a-ké*
    Ŋkpɛɛ́   he-said(Pst)

 (b) *jyɛɛ́*     *ɔ-jyɛ-ɛ*
  even-if    you-going(NonPst)

 (c)       *có*   *yɛ́*
        go(ImpImm) then

 (d) *nana*     *ŋ̆-kwɔ*   *mɛ́*
  now      I-begged(Pst) already

 (e)       *m̆-pwa*
        I-tired(Pst)

31(a) *có*
  go(ImpImm)

 (b) *mbɔgé*    *ɔ-gɛ-ne*    *nyíɛ* *menɔ*
  if      you-see(NonPst) later husband

 (c) *yi* *á-lá-pɔ́*      *ula*  *cuu* *ɛké* *me*
  who he-has-not(RelNonPstNeg) buttocks red like me

32(a)   *mendé* *a-bɔ́*    *unó* *bíí*
    wife she-took(Pst) things her

 (b)       *a-kulé*   *maáŋjyɛ*
        she-left(Pst) to-go

33(a) *ŋkpɛɛ́* *a-sɔ́*   *cwá cwá cwá* *né* *meti*
   Ŋkpɛɛ́ he-ran(Pst) [noise]   on way

          *wi*   *mewaá*
          which forest

 (b)       *a-jyɛ-táne*    *ne* *mbɛ* *meti*
        he-went-came-out(Pst) in front road

 (c)       *a-bɔ́*    *gela*
        he-took(Pst) climbing-rope

 (d)       *a-kwɔ́*   *megɔ*
        he-climbed(Pst) palm tree

 (e)       *a-lé-kɛ*   *uwuɔ́*
        he-Incep-cut(Pst) branches

34(a)   *mendé*  *a-tamé*
    wife    she-greeted(Pst)

 (b) *ŋkpɛɛ́*   *a-ké*  *wɔ* *waá*
  Ŋkpɛɛ́   he-said(Pst) you who

35(a)      *mendé*                *a-ké*             *me anyi    ŋkwɔ-ó*
           wife                   she-said(Pst)     I   Anyi   Ŋkwɔ-shouting

   (b)                            *n-jyɛ-ɛ-kéle*        *menɔ     yi      cá-ó*
                                  I-go-seek(NonPst)     husband  which   another

   (c) *ŋkpɛɛ́    ula*      *ú-gɛlé-ó*
       Ŋkpɛɛ́  buttocks   they-red(Attr) shouting

36(a)            *ŋkpɛɛ́*           *a-ké*
                 Ŋkpɛɛ́          he-said(Pst)

   (b)                            *pé*              *ame    wí      mfaá*
                                  look(ImpImm)     eyes   this    way-up

   (c)                            *ɔ́-gé-né*
                                  you-see-not(NonPstNeg)

   (d) *ɛba    ula*      *ú-gɛlé*
       mine   buttocks   they-red(Attr)

37         *Anyi*                 *a-koó*
           Anyi                   she-passed(Pst)

38(a) *ŋkpɛɛ́*                     *a-shulé*                    *wáwáwá*
      Ŋkpɛɛ́                    he-came-down(Pst)            quickly

   (b)                            *a-ma-jyé-sɔ́*                 *mewaá    mewaá*
                                  he-Rep-went-cut(Pst)         bush       bush

   (c)                            *a-jyɛ-táne*                  *mbɛ*
                                  he-went-came-out(Pst)        in front

   (d)                            *a-kwɔ́*             *mé         megɔ*
                                  he-climbed(Pst)    already    palm tree

   (e)                            *a-lé-kɛ*
                                  he-Incep-cut(Pst)

   (f) *mmyɛké*                   *a-kɛ-le*                *u-wuɔ́*
       as-if                      he-cuts(NonPst)         branches

39(a)      *mendé*                *a-cwɔ́*
           wife                   she-came(Pst)

   (b)                            *a-tamé*          *ji*
                                  she-greeted(Pst)  him

   (c)                            *a-kamé*           *wɔ    waá?*
                                  he-answered(Pst)  you    who?

40(a)                             *a-ké*
                                  she-said(Pst)

   (b) *me   Anyi*                *ŋkwɔ-ó*
       I    Anyi                  Ŋkwɔ-shouting

41                              *ɔ-jyɛ-ɛ*                    *ɛ́fɔ́*
                                you-going(NonPst)    where

42(a)                           *a-ké*
                                she-said(Pst)

   (b)                          *n-jyɛ-ɛ-kéle*              *menɔ*
                                I-going-look-for(NonPst)    husband
                                *yi cá*
                                another

   (c)                          *m̌-bá*           *menɔ*
                                I-married(Pst)    husband

   (d)            *yi*          *á-lá-pɔ́*                  *ula*       *ugɛ́lé*
                   who          he-has-not(RelAttrNeg)    buttocks    red

   (e) *meno      wa*
       husband    my
                   *yi*         *ḿ-ba-né*
                   that         I-married(RelPst)

   (f)                          *a-lu*          *ula*       *u-gɛ́lé*
                                he-is(Attr)    buttocks    red

43(a)                           *a-ké*
                                he-said(Pst)

   (b)                          *té-né*
                                be-standing(ImpAnyt)

   (c)                          *pé-lé*
                                be-looking-up(ImpAnyt)

   (d)                          *bwé-ɛ́*                   *a mɛ*    *mfaá*
                                he-lifting(ImpAnyt)    eyes      up

44(a)                           *a-fo*                    *ndeé*    *ula*
                                he-took-off(Pst)    cloth     buttocks

   (b)                          *a-ké*
                                he-said(Pst)

   (c)                          *ú-lú*               *mbɔ*         *ńnó*
                                they-are(Attr)    like-that    how

45(a)                           *a-ké*
                                she-said(Pst)

   (b)                          *ú-lú*       *ugɛ́lé*
                                they-are    red

46(a)                           *a-ké*
                                he-said(Pst)

(b) *pɔ́*                          *ɔ-ge*
    [excl]                        you-saw(Pst)

(c) *mala     sé    bɔ̌ŋkpɛɛ́ má-lu        magélé  magélé*
    buttocks  ours  Ŋkpɛɛ́ they-are(Attr)  red     red

47(a)                            *a-ké*
                                 he-said(Pst)

(b) *jyɛɛ́*                       *ɔ́-jyɛ́*                    *ɛ́fɔ́*
    even                         you-went(InsistImm)        where

(c) *jyɛɛ́   ndé   ŋkpɛɛ́  nne   ɔ́-jyɛ́-bá*
    even   what  Ŋkpɛɛ́ and   you-marry(InsistImm)

(d)                              *a-bɛ-ɛ*             *wiɛ́  ula      ugélé*
                                 he-will-be(NonPst)  just  buttocks  red

48(a)     *ayi   mendé   a-keré              yɛ́*
          the   wife    she-returned(Pst)   then

(b)                              *a-cwɔ-bá*                 *menɔ     wuú*
                                 she-came-married(Pst)     husband   her

49(a)                            *gɛ́*                 *ŋkaá   wú*
                                 see(ImpImm)          reason  why

(b) *ne*                         *á-jɔ́ɔ-ge*
    and                          they-say(RelNonPst)

(c) *ńnó   mala     bɔ̌ŋkpɛɛ́  má-lú            mámâ*
    how   buttocks  Ŋkpɛɛ́-pl. they-are(NonPst)  one

(d) *ne    ńtó    ńnó   refyá     ré-pwɔ          uto*
    and   also   how   cunning   it-more(Attr)   strength

**Free translation of text B**

Listen to a story! 2. We listen. 3. (a) See: (b) there was a man called
Ŋkpɛɛ́ [a species of monkey]; (c) he had (d) no wife. 4. (a) One day, he
got married (b) and came back. 5. (a-c) Both of them were living
together. 6. One day, he gave her some laws, 7. (a) He said, (b)
"Whenever I am sleeping in my room, (c) and you decide (d) to come
in, (e) do knock at the door. 8. Have you heard?" 9. The wife agreed.
10. (a) He gave another law (b) and said, (c) "Even at night when I
decide  (d) to sleep and you decide (f) to come into my room, (g) do not
carry  a lamp (h) along. 11. Have you heard?" 12. The wife agreed. 13.
One day, Ŋkpɛɛ́ went and drank wine and (b) was drunk; (c-d) he fell
asleep and (e) his cover fell off his buttocks. 14. (a) Ŋkpɛɛ́ had red buttocks, (b) and by those laws (c) he was trying  to conceal (d-e) from his
wife (f) this fact. 15. (a) But on that day, the wife forgot, (b) and so (c)
as she went in at  night (d) she carried a lamp. 16. (a) When (b) she

entered, (c) Ŋkpɛɛ́ had no cover on his buttocks. 17. (a) She saw (b) the husband's red buttocks. 18. (a) She shouted, (b) "So the man I married (c) has red buttocks! (d) Well, we shall see, I will abandon him." 19. She went and slept. 20. (a) The following morning she remained very moody; (b-c) her husband enquired (d) "My wife, what's the matter?" 21. (a) She said, (b) "So you have red buttocks (c-e) that you have been hiding from me. 22. (a) But yesterday I learned of it. (b) Our marriage is finished. (c) I am going away." 23. (a) Ŋkpɛɛ́ appeased her, (b) he gave her things (c) money, (d) and meat. 24. (a) The wife took these things and (b) stayed. 25. (a) Each time they had a little quarrel (b) she threatened (c) to leave, (d) questioning why she should be married to (e) a man who has red buttocks. 26. (a) She said (b) she was going away. 27. (a) Ŋkpɛɛ́ appeased her and (b) gave her things as before. 28. (a-c) Always appeasing her, (d) he became tired. 29. (a) One day, they had another quarrel. (b) She said (c) she was leaving. 30. (a) Ŋkpɛɛ́ said, (b) "If you want to leave, (c) you can do so. (d) I have appeased you often enough and (e) now I am tired. 31. (a) Go, then, (b) if you want to find a husband (c) who does not have red buttocks like me." 32. (a) The wife collected her things (b) and left. 33. (a) Ŋkpɛɛ́ took a path through the bush very quickly (b) and came out far ahead of her; (c) he took his climbing rope and (d) climbed a tall palm tree (e) and started cutting the branches. 34. (a) His wife greeted him. (b) Ŋkpɛɛ́ enquired, "Who are you?" 35. (a) She answered, "I am Anyi Nkwɔ. (b) I am going to look for another husband. (c) Ŋkpɛɛ́s buttocks have become red." 36. (a) Ŋkpɛɛ́ said (b-c) "Don't you see? (d) My buttocks are also red." 37. Anyi passed on. 38. (a) Ŋkpɛɛ́ came down very quickly, (b) again took a bush path, and (c) came out ahead. (d) He climbed a tall palm tree. (e) He started cutting. (f) He was pretending to cut palm branches. 39. (a) The wife came (b) and greeted him. (c) He answered and enquired who the person was. 40. (a) She said, (b) "I am Anyi Nkwɔ." 41. "Where are you going?" 42. (a) She said, (b) "I am going to look for another husband, (c-d) a husband who does not have red buttocks. (e) The man I married (f) has red buttocks." 43. (a) He said, (b) "Remain standing. (c) Look up. (d) Lift up your eyes." 44. (a) He took off the cover from his buttocks (b) and said, (c) "How are they?" 45. (a) She answered, (b) "They are red." 46. (a) He commented, (b) "Did you see? (c) All of us ŋkpɛɛ́ have red buttocks." 47. (a) He added, (b) "Wherever you go, (c) whoever you marry (d) will have red buttocks." 48. (a) So the wife returned home (b) and stayed happily with her husband. 49. (a) That is why (b) it is said (c) that all ŋkpɛɛ́ have red buttocks (d) and that cleverness is more than strength.

**TEXT C How to Make a Sleeping Mat**

1(a) *mbɔgé*          *n-jɔ́-gé*
    if          I-said(Cond)

(b) *ńnó*          *n-cwɔ-ɔ-jó*          *gébɔ̂*
    that          I-come-weave(NonPst)  mat

(c)          *ň-kpé*          *mewaá*
              I-entered(Pst)          forest

(d)          *ň-sɔ́*          *ŋkó*
              I-cut(Pst)          reed

(e)          *ň-kpá*
              I-carried(Pst)

(f)          *ň-cwɔ́*          *ne      éjí    mmu*
              I-came(Pst)          with    it    home

2(a)          *n-cwɔ-gé*
              I-came(Cond)

(b)          *m̌-feé*          *meshií*
              I-removed(Pst)          thorns

(c)          *m̌-feé*
              I-removed(Pst)

(d)          *m̌-feé*
              I-removed(Pst)

(e)          *ň-kpá*          *yé      éjí*
              I-carried(Pst)          then    it

(f)          *ŋm̌-ŋme*          *ŋmŋmɛɛ́*
              I-threw(Pst)          sun

3(a)          *ŋm-ŋme-gé*          *ŋmŋmɛɛ́*
    (if)          I-threw(Cond)          sun

(b)          *é-kpɛá*
              they-whiten(Attr)

4(a)          *é-kpɛá-gé*          *yé*
    (if)          they-whiten(Cond)      then

(b)          *m̌-bɔ́*          *anɔ*
              I-took(Pst)          males

(c)          *ň-gyá*
              I-split(Pst)

(d)          #          *agiέ*
                        females

(e)          *ň-gyá*
              I-split(Pst)

| | | |
|---|---|---|
| 5(a) | *ŋ̌-kwɔ* | *ɛpo* |
| | I-ground(Pst) | camwood |
| (b) | *ň-sɛ* | *anɔ    bímbɔ* |
| | I-took(Pst) | males  those |
| (c) | *m̌-fyɛ́* | *mesɛɛ́* |
| | I-put(Pst) | pot |
| (d) | *ň-cwɛ́* | *manaá* |
| | I-fetched(Pst) | water |
| (e) | *m̌-fyɛ́* | |
| | I-put(Pst) | |
| (f) | *m̌-bɔ́* | *ɛpo       wirmbɔ* |
| | I-took(Pst) | camwood  that |
| (g) | *m-fyɛ́* | *wiɛ́* |
| | I-put(Pst) | there |
| (h) | *n-tyɛɛ́* | *mewɛ* |
| | I-put-on(Pst) | fire |
| 6(a) | *n-tyɛɛ-gé* | *mewɛ* |
| (if) | I-put-on(Cond) | fire |
| (b) | *é-nyɛ́* | *mbaá    ŋko* |
| | they-stained(Pst) | place   reed |
| 7 *ŋkó yímbɔ* | *é-la* | *cuu* |
| reed   that | they-remained(Pst) | red |
| 8(a) | *ŋ-gya-gé* | *ɛyí    pópé* |
| | I-split(Cond) | the   white |
| (b) | *m̌-ʃyɛ́* | |
| | I-put(Pst) | |
| (c) | *m̌-bɔ́* | *ɛyí   megélé yimbɔ* |
| | I-took(Pst) | the   red      thcrc |
| (d) | *m̌-ʃyɛ́* | |
| | I-put(Pst) | |
| (e) | *ň-lɔ* | *yɛ    mǎnjo* |
| | I-started(Pst) | then   to-weave |
| 9(a) | *ŋ-koo-ge* | *ŋkó* |
| | I-pass(NonPst) | strand |
| (b) | *m̌-bɔ́* | *ŋkó* |
| | I-took(Pst) | strand(reed) |
| (c) | *ŋ-koo-ge* | *ŋkó* |
| | I-pass(NonPst) | strand(reed) |

(d)                             *m̌-bɔ́*                         *ŋkó*
                                I-took(Pst)                    strand(reed)

10(a)                           *n-jo-gé*                       *ɛyígé   mbɔ   kpáá*
    (if)                        I-weave(Cond)                  that    for    long

  (b)                           *ň̩-ké*
                                I-said(Pst)

  (c)                           *m-fyɛ-ɛ*                       *mansá*
                                I-put(NonPst)                  design

11(a)                           *ň-cwɔ́*
                                I-came(Pst)

  (b)                           *m̌-fyɛ́*                        *mansá*
                                I-put(Pst)                     design

  (c)                           *m̌-fyɛ́*                        *malɔ   mansá*
                                I-put(Pst)                     lines   design
                                                               *áléɛ́*
                                                               three

  (d)                           *m̌-má-m̌-bɔ́*                    *ɛyígé   pópó*
                                I-Rep-I-took(Pst)              that    white

  (e)                           *ň̩-gbɛ́*                        *né   mbɛ*
                                I-closed(Pst)                  in   front

12(a)                           *m-bɔ-ɔ*                        *ɛyígé   mbɔ*
                                I-take(NonPst)                 that    one

  (b)                                                           *ɛyígé   mbɔ*
                                                               that    one

  (c)                                                           *ɛyígé   mbɔ*
                                                               that    one

13(a) *ubá*                     *ú-kwé*           *ulɛɛ́*
      spots                     they-fell(Pst)   three

  (b)                                                           *ɛbí   pópó   úpéá*
                                                               those  white  two

  (c)                                                           *ɛyígé   mansá   gémâ*
                                                               that    design  one

14    *ɛyígé   mbɔ   ne   á-kú-u*                              *gebo   mansá*
      that    one   and  they-call(RelNonPst)                 mat    design

15(a)                           *á-la-bɔ́*
                                they-Hab-took(Pst)

  (b)                           *á-bɛle-ge*                     *wié*
                                they-sleep(NonPst)             there

**Free translation of text C**

1. (a) If I decided (b) to weave a sleeping mat, (c) I would go into the forest, (d) cut reed, (e) and carry it (f) home. 2. (a) Having come home, (b-d) I would remove the thorns, (e) carry it out, and (f) spread it in the sun. 3. (a) Spread in the sun, (b) the material becomes white. 4. (a) When it is white, (b-c) I split it into males (d-e) and females. 5. (a) I grind camwood, (b) then I take the males, (c) and put them in the pot, (d) put water in it, (e-f) add the camwood, (g) and place the pot (h) on the fire. 6. (a) Put on the fire, (b) the material is dyed. 7. The material becomes red. 8. (a) When I split the white material, (b) I put it aside. (c-d) I also add the red ones (e) and then start weaving. 9. (a) I skip one strand and (b) pick one. (c) I skip one (d) and pick the next. 10. (a) Having woven that style, (b) I decide (c) to add a new design. 11. (a) I decided (b) to put on the design, (c) three bands of design; (d) then again I add the white band (e) to close in the red. 12. (a) I weave that one (the white) (b-c) for a long time. 13. (a) Now there are three bands, (b) two white ones and (c) a red. 14. That is what is called a sleeping mat with a design. 15. (a) It can now be used (b) for sleeping on.

**TEXT D Ŋgbɛ Society**

| 1(a) *ŋgbɛ ŋgbɛ* | *a-lu* | *lé* | *uka* | *ande* |
|---|---|---|---|---|
| Ngbe | it-is(Attr) | Foc | organization | men |
| (b) *mendé* | *ǎ-jyé-ɛ́* | | *wiɛ́* | |
| woman | she-goes-not(NonPstNeg) | | there | |
| (c) *ande bífɔ́* | *á-pɔ́* | | *wiɛ́* | |
| men  some | are-not(AttrNeg) | | there | |
| 2(a) *ŋgbɛ* | *a-lu* | *uka* | | |
| Ngbe | it-is(Attr) | organization | | |
| (b) *bí* | *ú-kwyɛ́ɛ-ge* | | *melɔ* | |
| which | it-makes-good(RelNonPst) | | village | |
| 3(a) | *a-wia* | *mabɛ́* | | |
|  | it-has(Attr) | laws | | |
| (b) *yí* | *á-pyé-ɛ* | | *melɔ* | |
| which | they-make(RelNonPst) | | village | |
| (c) | *ɛ́-kɛ́-ne* | | *cáncá* | |
|  | it-moves(RelNonPst) | | well | |
| 4(a) *jyɛɛ́* | *ɔ-lu* | | *wiɛ́* | |
| even-if | you-are(Attr) | | there | |
| (b) *jyɛɛ́* | *ɔ́-pɔ́* | | *wiɛ́* | |
| even-if | you-are-not(AttrNeg) | | there | |

(c) *ne*                          *ó-kwe-né*              *ébé  ŋgbɛ*
   and                          you-fell(RelPst)    law   of-Ngbɛ

(d)                               *á-nyé*                 *wɔ*
                    they-ate(Pst)    you

5(a) *né  ŋgbɛ  bɔɔ*              *akoako  á-pɔ*                        *gefɔɔ*
    in   Ngbɛ   people         all     they-are-not(AttrNeg)   kind
                     *gema*
                     one

  (b) *afwa*                      *á-lú*
      chiefs                      they-are(Attr)

  (c) *bɔɔ*        *retú*           *á-lú*                *ntó  wié*
      people      nothing          they-are(Attr)        also   there

6(a) *muú      yi*                *a-lu*       *mfwa  ŋgbɛ  meko*
    person   who              he-is(Attr)   chief  Ngbɛ   all

  (b)                              *á-ku-u*                  *ji     tátá*
                  they-call(NonPst)    him    tata

7(a)    *ji*                      *a-jɔɔ-gé*
    (if) him                      he-speaks(Cond)

  (b)                              *é-byé*
                  they-finished(Pst)

8(a) *muú      yi*                *á-lá-pɔ*                    *né  ŋgbɛ*
    person   who              he-is-not(RelNeg)    in   Ngbɛ

  (b) *ne*                       *a-jɔɔ-gé*
      but                       he-decided(Cond)

  (c) *ńnó*                      *a-jyɛ-ɛ gé*
      that                      he-going-see(NonPst)

  (d)                              *a-kpá*            *mmɔɔ  dɔɔ*
                  he-took(Pst)    wine     much

  (e)                              *a-fé*            *ne   mámi*
                  he-went(Pst)    with    it

9(a)                               *a-cyɛé*          *ŋka*
                  he-gave(Pst)    money

  (b)                              *a-cyɛé*          *menya*
                  he-gave(Pst)    meat

10(a)                              *a-cyɛ-gé*          *mbɔ*
    (if)                             he-gave(Cond)    like-that

  (b)                              *á-lɛré*                  *ji    ŋgbɛ*
                  they-showed(Pst)    him    Ngbɛ

| 11(a)          |           | ɔbɛ-gé              |          | mé          | muú     | ŋgbɛ    |
|                |           | you-are(Cond)       |          | already     | person  | Ngbɛ    |
| (b) jyɛέ       |           | ɔ́-jyɛ-έ            |          |             | ndé     | melɔ    |
| even-if        |           | you-who-went(RelPst)|          |             | what    | village |
| (c) ɛwí        | ŋgbɛ      | á-lú                |          |             |         |         |
| which          | Ngbɛ      | it-is(Attr-Rel)     |          |             |         |         |
| (d)            |           | ɔ-kpɛ-ne            |          | wiέ         | retú    |         |
|                |           | you-go-in(NonPst)   |          | there       | nothing |         |
|                |           |                     |          |             |         |         |
| 12(a) ŋgbɛ     |           | a-ja                | ucu      | dɔ́ɔ́       |         |         |
| Ngbɛ           |           | it-had(Pst)         | aspects  | much        |         |         |
| (b)            |           | n-jɔɔ-gé            |          |             |         |         |
| (if)           |           | I-said(Cond)        |          |             |         |         |
| (c) ńnó        |           | ŋ-gare-ge           | reko     |             |         |         |
| that           |           | I-tell(NonPst)      | all      |             |         |         |
| (d)            |           | de-bɛle-ge          |          | fa          | fi      |         |
|                |           | we-sleep(NonPst)    |          | here        | today   |         |
|                |           |                     |          |             |         |         |
| 13(a) ɛkέkέ wí |           | ḿ-bɔ-ɔ́             |          | mǎŋgaré     | wɔ      |         |
| little   that  |           | I-took(RelPst)      |          | to tell     | you     |         |
| (b)            |           | έ-byέ               |          | mbɔ         |         |         |
|                |           | they-finished(Pst)  |          | like-that   |         |         |

**Free translation of text D**

1. (a) Ngbɛ is an organization for men; (b) women are not allowed there. (c) There are also certain men who are not members. 2. (a) Ngbɛ is an organization (b) that works for the good of the village. 3. (a) It has laws (b) which make the village (c) go well. 4. (a) Whether you are a member (b) or not, (c) once you break one of the laws of this organization (d) you are fined. 5. (a) In this organization, not everybody is of the same rank; (b) there are lords and (c) there are the commoners. 6. (a) The person who is the head of this organization (b) is called *tata*. 7. (a) Once he speaks (b) it is final. 8. (a) A person who is not a member, (b) but decides (c) to become one, (d) takes much wine (e) to it. 9. (a) He gives money and (b) meat. 10. (a) Having given these, (b) he is shown how the organization is. 11. (a) Once you are a member, (b) wherever you go (c) if the organization exists there, (d) you are admitted freely to it. 12. (a) There are many aspects of this organization; (b) if I were to decide (c) to recount everything about it, (d) we would spend the whole day and night here today. 13. (a) The little that I had to tell you (b) is now finished.

**TEXT E: Always Do Your Work Well**

1(a) *Negbo,*               *cwɔ́*          *wi*
     Negbo              come(ImpImm)   this-way

  (b)               *jwɔ́lé*         *ka*
                     sit(ImpImm)   down

  (c)               *m̌-bɔ́*     *ɛkɛ̂kɛ́*   *mecɔ́*   *maánjɔ́*
                   I-took(Pst)  little    speech   to-say

2(a)                *gɛ́*        *wɔ*   *mbɔ*
                   see(ImpImm)  you  like-that

  (b)               *ɔ́-jyɛ́-ɛ*              *malɔ*
                   you-who-going(RelNonPst)  towns
               *bɔɔ́*    *cácá*
               people   other

  (c) *muú*    *se*   *wiɛ́*   *á-pɔ́*
     person   our   there   he-is-not(AttrNeg)

3    *utɔɔ́*   *mekálá*    *ne*    *ɔ́-jyɛ́-ɛ-pyɛ́*
     work    white-man   that   you-going-do(RelNonPst)

4(a)              *ɔ-jyɛ-gé*
   (if)           you-go(Cond)

  (b)               *ɔ-pyɛ-ɛ*       *wiɛ́*   *ú-bí*
                   you-do(NonPst)  there  it

5(a) *muú*    *kpa* *wiɛ́*   *ne*    *á-ku-ú*        *wɔ*
     person  big   there   that   he-called(RelPst)  you

  (b)               *ɔ̌-kamé*        *sa*
                   you-answered(Pst)  sir

  (c) *sa*   *sa*   *yimbɔ*  *ǎ-pyɛ́-ɛ́*         *genó*
     sir   sir   who    it-makes-not(NonPst)  nothing

6(a)             *ɔ-jyɛ-gé*     *ɛwu*
   (if)           you-go(Cond)  there

  (b)              *ɔ-gbare-ge*      *metɔɔ́*  *wíɛ*
                 you-hold(NonPst)  heart  your

7(a) *mendé*  *muú*   *ɔ́-ka-gé*
     wife     person  you-dare-not(ImpNeg)

  (b)             *ɔ́-kwɔ́lé*
              you-follow(InsistImm)

8(a) *mendé*  *muú*   *a-lu*       *geŋkwɔ́*  *ge*  *ŋmŋme*
     wife     person  she-is(Attr)  carcass  of  goat

(b)                                   ɔ-kpa-gé
  (if)                               you-carried(Cond)

(c) mbɔɔ́                          ǎ-gɔ́-ɔ́-nyíɛ               wɔ    mǎŋgií
  owner                          he-leave-not(NonPstNeg)    you    to-ask

9(a) mendé    nekɛ   a-lu          geŋkwɔ́ ge menya
  women    travel   she-is(Attr)   carcass   of   animal

  (b) jyɛɛ́                           ɔ́-kpá
    even-if                        you-carried(Pst)

  (c) muú     fɔ     á-gí-í-gé                      wɔ
    person   some   he-asks-not(NonPstNeg)   you

10(a) ne                          gé
   but                          see(ImpImm)

  (b) bɔɔ́    kpa    dɔɔ́   á-gbó          gétuí     gé   andé
    people   most   many   they-died(Pst)   because   of   women

  (c)                                          wuí
                                           listen(ImpImm)

11     mendé   muú   ɔ́-fyɛ-gé                ame   wié
   wife       person   you-put-not(ImpNeg)   eyes   there

12(a)                              ɔ́-jyɛ́-ɛ                mbɔ
   (as)                          you-going(RelNonPst)   like-that

  (b)                              ɔ́-ka-gé
                              you-dare-not(ImpNeg)

  (c)                              ɔ́-bá                      mendé melɔ   cá
                              you-marry(InsistImm) wife    village other

  (d)                              ɔ-ba-gé                  mendé melɔ    cá
   (if)                          you-marry(Cond)   wife    village   other

  (e)                              ɔ̌-la                       meŋkɛɛ́ melɔ   wíɛ
                              you-remained(Pst)   stranger   home   your

  (f) baá    bíɛ   á-jɔɔ́-gé-nyíɛ                         sê      dényá
    children   your   they-speak-not(NonPstNeg)         longer   Dényá

13     ɛsé   bína   de-jɔɔ ge          ndé   mejɔɔ́   né   ebwɔ́
   we   these   we-speak(NonPst)   what   language   to   them

14(a)                              ɔ-bɛlé-gé               kpaá
   (when)                        you-slept(Cond)   long

  (b)                              ɔ̌-cwɔ́
                              you-came(Pst)

  (c)                              ɔ̌-pɛ                     ɛsé
                              you-looked(Pst)   us

15          *ɔ́-jü-gé*             *nte*     *melɔ*
                  you-forget-not(ImpNeg)   thought   home

16(a)       *ɔ-jyɛ-gé*
     (when)      you-go(Cond)

     (b)        *pyé-gé*         *utɔ́*   *bíɛ*   *cáncá*
                 be-doing(ImpAnyt)   work   your   well

     (c)        *ɔ́-kɛlé-gé*       *mejɔ́*
                 you-seek-not(ImpNeg)   trouble

     (d)        *ɔ́-nyu-gé*        *mmɔ́*   *dɔ́ɔ́*
                 you-drink-not(ImpNeg)   wine   much

   (e) *mmcɔ́*   *dɔ́ɔ́*   *ma-pyɛ-ɛ*
     wine    much   it-makes(NonPst)

   (f) *ŋka*        *é-bé-é*         *wɔ*   *amu*
     money     it-is-not(NonPstNeg)   you   hands

17(a)       *kɛ*       *pere*
                 walk(ImpImm)   well

     (b)        *ɔ́-jü-gé*         *nte*
                 you-forget-not(ImpNeg)   thought

     (c) *ɛtíré*    *ń-jɔ-ɔ́*     *mbɔ*
       those     I-said(RelPst)   like-that

     (d)        *jwɔ́-lé*        *cáncá*
                 be-staying(ImpAnyt)   well

     (e)        *pyé-gé*        *ńtó*   *utɔ́*   *cáncá*
                 be-doing(ImpAnyt)   also   work   well

     (f) *ɛwa*       *é-byɛ́*       *mbɔ*
       mine     they-finished(Pst)   like-that

**Free translation of text E**

1. (a) Negbo, come here, (b) sit down; (c) I have something to tell you.
2. (a) There you are, (b) about to leave for foreign lands (c) where none of our people are. 3. It is white man's work you are going to do. 4. (a) Once there (b) you should always be doing your work. 5. (a) If your boss calls you, (b) answer respectfully; (c) you lose nothing by being respectful. 6. (a) Once there, (b) you should always comport yourself well. 7. (a) Dare not (b) lust after anybody's wife. 8. (a) A wife is like the carcass of a goat; (b) if you carry it off, (c) the owner will definitely come for it. 9. (a) A free woman is like the carcass of a forest animal; (b) if you claim it, (c) nobody will question you. 10. (a) Please note well, (b) many people have died because of women. (c) Listen to this! 11. Do not be attracted to anybody's wife. 12. (a) As you are going, (b) dare not (c)

marry a foreign woman; (d) if you marry a foreign woman, (e) you remain a stranger in your own land; (f) your children will no longer speak Dényá. 13. What language can we use with them then? 14. (a) After some time (b) you should come and (c) visit us. 15. Never forget home. 16. (a) Once there, (b) be doing your work well; (c) don't look for trouble, (d) don't drink a lot (e-f) because much drinking makes you poor. 17. (a) Go well; (b) don't forget (c) what I have said. (d) Stay well; (e) be doing your work well. (f) That is all I had to say.

# Bibliography

Anderson, John M. 1971. *The Grammar of Case: Towards a Localistic Theory*. Cambridge Studies in Linguistics, vol. 4. Cambridge: University Press.

Anderson, Stephen C. 1980. Tense/Aspect in Ngyembɔɔn-Bamileke. Paper presented to the 14th Annual Congress of West African Linguistic Society, 14–18 April, at Cotonou.

Anon. 1976. How Many Are We? Help Us Count You. *General Population and Housing Census*. Yaoundé: Ministry of Economic Planning.

Ansre, Gilbert. 1966. The Verbid: A Caveat to 'Serial Verbs'. *Journal of West African Languages* 3:29–32.

Awobuluyi, A.D. 1973. The Modifying Serial Construction: A Critique. *Studies in African Linguistics* 4:87–111.

Aukema, T., and W. Dagny. 1979. The Relation between Chronological and Logical Order in Tamajeq Overlay. MS.

Bamgbose, Ayo. 1973. The Modifying Serial Construction: A Reply. *Studies in African Linguistics* 4:207–18.

————. 1974. On Serial Verbs and Verbal Status. *Journal of West African Languages* 9:17–48.

————. 1980. Issues in the Analysis of Serial Verb Constructions. Paper presented to the 14th Annual Congress of West African Linguistic Society, 14–18 April at Cotonou.

Bearth, Ilse. 1978. Discourse Patterns in Toura Folk Tales. In *Papers on Discourse*, ed by Joseph E.Grimes, 208–25. SIL Publications in Linguistics and Related Fields, 51. Dallas, Texas: Summer Institute of Linguistics.

Bearth, Thomas. 1971. *L'énoncé Toura (Côte d'Ivoire)*. SIL Publications in

Linguistics and Related Fields, 30. Norman, Oklahoma: Summer Institute of Linguistics of the University of Oklahoma.

Beekman, John, and John Callow. 1974. *Translating the Word of God.* Grand Rapids, Michigan: Zondervan.

Bendor-Samuel, John T. 1968. Verb Clusters in Izi. *Journal of West African Languages* 5:119–28.

Bieri, Dora and Marlene Schulze. 1973. An approach to discourse in Sunwar. In *Clause, Sentence, and Discourse Patterns in Selected Languages of Nepal, Part 1, General Approach*, ed. by Austin Hale, 401–62. SIL Publications in Linguistics and Related Fields, 40. Norman, Oklahoma: Summer Institute of Linguistics of the University of Oklahoma.

Binam Bikoi, C., and E. Soundjock. 1977 *Les Contes du Cameroun.* Yaoundé : Centre d'Edition et de Production de Manuels et d'Auxiliaires de l'Enseignement.

Callow, Kathleen. 1974. *Discourse Considerations in Translating the Word of God.* Grand Rapids, Michigan: Zondervan.

Chafe, Wallace L. 1970. *Meaning and the Structure of Language.* Chicago: University of Chicago Press.

Chapman, R. 1974. *Linguistics and Literature: An Introduction to Literary Stylistics.* Reprint of 1973 ed. with corrections. London: Edward Arnold.

Chia, E.N. 1976. Kom Tenses and Aspects. Ph.D. dissertation, Georgetown University, Washington, D.C.

———. 1982. Aspects as Verbs. *Cahiers du département des langues africaines et linguistique* 2:73–93, Yaoundé: Université.

Chomsky, Noam. 1957. *Syntactic Structures.* The Hague: Mouton.

Cook, Walter A. 1971. Improvements in Case Grammar, 1970. *Language and Linguistics/Working Papers* 2:10–22.

Coulthard, Malcolm. 1975. Discourse Analysis in English – A Short Review of the Literature. In *Language Teaching and Linguistics: Abstracts* 8:2.73–89. Cambridge: University Press.

———. 1977. *An Introduction to Discourse Analysis.* London: Longman.

Crabb, David W. 1965. *Ekoid Bantu Languages of Ogoja, Eastern Nigeria. Part 1: Introduction, phonology and comparative vocabulary.* West African Languge Monographs, 4. Cambridge: University Press.

Crystal, David, and Derek Davy. 1969. *Investigating English Style.* London: Longman (reprinted 1973).

Fillmore, C. J. 1968. The Case for Case. In *Universals in Linguistic Theory,* ed. by Emmon Bach and Robert T. Harms, 1–88. New York: Holt, Rinehart and Winston.

Forster, Keith. 1977. The Narrative Folklore Discourse in Border Cuna. In *Discourse Grammar: Studies in Indigenous Languages of Colombia, Panama, and Ecuador, Part 2*, ed. by Robert E. Longacre and Frances Woods, 1–23. Dallas, Texas: Summer Institute of Linguistics and the University of Texas at Arlington.

George, Isaac. 1976. Verb Serialization and Lexical Decomposition. *Studies in African Linguistics*, Supplement 6:63–72.

Gleason, H.A., Jr. 1961. *An Introduction to Descriptive Linguistics*. Rev. ed. New York: Holt, Rinehart and Winston.

———. 1968. Contrastive Analysis in Discourse Structure. In *Report of the 19th Annual Round Table Meeting on Linguistics and Language Studies*, ed. by James E. Alatis, 39–63. Washington, D.C.: Georgetown University Press.

Greenberg, Joseph H., ed. 1963. *Languages of Africa*. The Hague: Mouton

Gregory, M., and S. Carrol. 1978. *Language and Situation: Language Varieties and Their Social Contexts*. London: Routledge and Kegan Paul.

Grimes, Joseph E. 1972. Outlines and Overlays. *Language* 48:513–24.

———. 1975. *The Thread of Discourse*. Janua Linguarum, series minor, 207. The Hague: Mouton.

———, ed. 1978a. *Papers on Discourse*. SIL Publications in Linguistics and Related Fields, 51. Dallas, Texas: Summer Institute of Linguistics and the University of Texas at Arlington.

———. 1978b. Narrative Studies in Oral Texts. In *Current Trends in Textlinguistics*, ed. by W.U. Dressler, 123–32. Berlin: Walter de Gruyter.

Guthrie, Malcolm. 1948. *The Classification of the Bantu Languages. Handbook of African Languages*. London: International African Institute. Reprint in 1967. London: Dawsons of Pall Mall.

Hale, Austin. 1973. Toward the Systematization of Display Grammar. In *Clause, Sentence, and Discourse Patterns in Selected Languages of Nepal*, ed. by Austin Hale, 1–37. SIL Publications in Linguistics and Related Fields, 40. Norman, Oklahoma: Summer Institute of Linguistics of the University of Oklahoma.

———. 1974. On the Systematization of Box 4. In *Advances in Tagmemics*, ed. by Ruth M. Brend, 55–74. Amsterdam: North Holland Publishing Company.

Halliday, M.A.K. 1970. Language Structure and Language Functions. In *New Horizons in Linguistics*, ed. by John Lyons, 140–65. Harmondsworth, Middlesex, England: Penguin Books.

———. 1973. *Explorations in the Functions of Language*. London: Edward Arnold.

Halliday, M.A.K., and Ruqaiya Hasan. 1976. *Cohesion in English*. London: Longman.

Harris, Zellig S. 1963. *Discourse Analysis Reprints*. The Hague: Mouton.

Heine, B. 1976. *A Typology of African Languages*. Berlin: Dietrich Reimer.

Hyman, Larry M. 1975. *Phonology Theory and Analysis*. New York: Holt, Rinehart and Winston.

Johnston, Harry H. 1919 and 1922. *A Comparative Study of the Bantu and Semi-Bantu Languages*. 2 vols. Oxford: Clarendon Press.

Jordan, Dean L. 1978. Nafaara Tense-Aspect in the Folk Tale. In *Papers on Discourse*, ed by Joseph E.Grimes, 84–90. SIL Publications in Linguistics and Related Fields, 51. Dallas, Texas: Summer Institute of Linguistics.

Krüsi, Martin, and Dorothee Krüsi. 1978. The Use of Modes in Chiquitano Discourse. In *Work Papers of the Summer Institute of Linguistics*. Riberalta, Bolivia 1972–76:95–162.

Leech, Geoffrey, and Jan Svartvik. 1975. *A Communicative Grammar of English*. London: Longman.

Leroy, Jacqueline. 1977. *Morphologie et classes nominales en mankon*. Paris: SELAF.

*Linguistic Survey of the Northern Bantu Borderland*, vol. 1. 1956. London: Oxford University Press (for the International African Institute).

Longacre, Robert E. 1968. *Discourse, Paragraph, and Sentence Structure in Selected Philippine Languages*, vol. 1. Santa Ana, California: Summer Institute of Linguistics.

———. 1972. *Hierarchy and Universality of Discourse Constituents in New Guinea Lanaguages*. 2 vols. Washington, D.C.: Georgetown University Press.

———. 1974. Narrative versus Other Discourse Genre. In *Advances in Tagmemics*, ed. by Ruth M. Brend, 357–76. Amsterdam: North Holland.

———. 1976. *An Anatomy of Speech Notions*. Lisse: Peter de Ridder Press.

———. 1977. Discourse Analysis and Literacy. In *Language and Literacy:*

*Current Issues and Research*, ed. by Thomas P. Gorman, 71–87. Tehran, Iran: International Institute for Adult Literacy Methods.

———— and S. Levinsohn. 1978. Field Analysis of Discourse. In *Current Trends in Textlinguistics*, ed. by W.U. Dressler, 103–22. Berlin: Walter de Gruyter.

Lyons, John. 1968. *Introduction to Theoretical Linguistics*. Cambridge: University Press.

————. 1977. *Semantics 2*. Cambridge: University Press.

Mansfeld, Alfred. 1908. *Urwald-Dokumente*. Berlin: Dietrich Reimer (Ernst Vohsen).

Marchese, Lynell. 1978. Time Reference in Godié. In *Papers on Discourse*, ed by Joseph E.Grimes, 63–75. SIL Publications in Linguistics and Related Fields, 51. Dallas, Texas: Summer Institute of Linguistics.

Newman, Bonnie. 1978. The Longuda Verb. In *Papers on Discourse*, ed by Joseph E.Grimes, 25–45. SIL Publications in Linguistics and Related Fields, 51. Dallas, Texas: Summer Institute of Linguistics.

Newton, Dennis. 1978. Guarayu Discourse. In *Work Papers of the Summer Institute of Linguistics*. Riberalta, Bolivia 1972–76, 163–269.

Palmer, F.R. 1965. A *Linguistic Study of the English Verb*. London: Longman.

Pike, Kenneth L. 1967. *Language in Relation to a Unified Theory of the Structure of Human Behavior*. 2nd rev. ed. The Hague: Mouton.

————. 1970. *Tagmemic and Matrix Linguistics Applied to Selected African Languages*. SIL Publications in Linguistics and Related Fields, 23. Norman, Oklahoma: Summer Institute of Linguistics of the University of Oklahoma.

———— and Evelyn Pike. 1982. *Grammatical Analysis*. Rev. ed. Summer Institute of Linguistics Publications in Linguistics, 53. Dallas, Texas: Summer Institute of Linguistics and the University of Texas at Arlington.

Platt, John T. 1971. *Grammatical Form and Grammatical Meaning: A Tagmemic View of Fillmore's Deep Structure Case Concepts*. Amsterdam: North Holland.

Robinson, C. 1979. Participants in Gunu Narrative Discourse. MS.

Salone, Sukari. 1979. Typology of Conditionals and Conditionals in Haya. *Studies in African Linguistics*. Special Issue on Bantu Syntax 10:1.65–80.

Stanley, Carol. 1982. Form and Function of Adjectival Elements in Tikar. *Journal of West African Languages* 12:83–94.

Talbot, Percy A. 1926. *The Peoples of Southern Nigeria. Vol. 4, Linguistics and Statistics*. London: Oxford University Press.

Trithart, Lee. 1979. Topicality: An Alternative to the Relational View of Bantu Passive. *Studies in African Linguistics: Special Issue on Bantu Syntax* 10:1.1–30.

Tyhurst, James J. 1983. *Linguistic Survey of the Nyang Languages*. Yaoundé: Société International de Linguistique.

Tyhurst, J.J. and J.L. Tyhurst. 1983. *Sociolinguistic Survey of Kenyang and Denya*. Yaoundé: Société Internationale de Linguistique.

Weinrich, H. 1973. *Le Temps*. Paris: Editions du Seuil.

Welmers, William E. 1973. African Language Structures. Berkeley: University of California Press.

Westermann, Dietrich and Margaret A. Bryan. 1952. *Languages of West Africa*. Part 2 of the Handbook of African Languages. London: Oxford University Press (for the International African Institute). Reprint in 1970. London: Dawsons of Pall Mall.

Wienold, G. 1978. Textlinguistic Approaches to Written Works of Art. In *Current Trends in Textlinguistics*, ed. by W.U. Dressler. Berlin: Walter de Gruyter.

Wiesemann, Ursula. 1980a. Events and Non-Events in Kaingáng Discourse. *In Wege zur Universalienforschung: sprachwissen-schaftliche Beiträge zum 60 Geburtstag von Hansjakob Seiler*, ed. by Gunter Brettschneider and Christian Lehmann, 419–33. Tubingen: Gunter Narr.

———. 1980b. *Native Speaker Reaction and the Development of Writing Systems for Unwritten Languages*. Cahiers du département des langues africaines et linguistique 1. Yaoundé: Université.

———, Etienne Sadembouo and M. Tadadjeu. 1983. Guide pour le *Développement des systemes d'écriture des langues africaines*. Collection PROPELCA 2. Yaoundé: Université.

Williamson, Kay. 1971. The Benue-Congo Languages and Ijo. In *Current Trends in Linguistics*, vol. 7: Linguistics in Sub-Saharan Africa, ed. by Thomas A. Sebeok, 245–306. The Hague: Mouton.

# SUMMER INSTITUTE OF LINGUISTICS
## Publications in Linguistics

(* = in microfiche only  ** = also in microfiche)

1. **Comanche Texts** by E. Canonge (1958) *
2. **Pocomchi Texts** by M. Mayers (1958) *
3. **Mixteco Texts** by A. Dyk (1959) *
4. **A Synopsis of English Syntax** by E. A. Nida (1960) *
5. **Mayan Studies I** by W. C. Townsend et al. (1960) *
6. **Sayula Popoluca Texts, with Grammatical Outline** by L. Clark (1961) *
7. **Studies in Ecuadorian Indian Languages I** by C. Peeke et al. (1962) *
8. **Totontepec Mixe Phonotagmemics** by J. C. Crawford (1963) *
9. **Studies in Peruvian Indian Languages I** by M. Larson et al. (1963) *
10. **Verb Studies in Five New Guinea Languages** by A. Pence et al. (1964) *
11. **Some Aspects of the Lexical Structure of a Mazatec Historical Text** by G. M. Cowan (1965) *
12. **Chatino Syntax** by K. Pride (1965) *
13. **Chol Texts on the Supernatural** by V. Warkentin (1965) *
14. **Phonemic Systems of Colombian Languages** by V. G. Waterhouse et al. (1967) *
15. **Bolivian Indian Tribes: Classification, Bibliography and Map of Present Language Distribution** by H. and M. Key (1967) *
16. **Bolivian Indian Grammars I and II** by E. Matteson et al. (1967) *
17. **Totonac: from Clause to Discourse** by A. Reid et al. (1968) *
18. **Tzotzil Grammar** by M. M. Cowan (1969) *
19. **Aztec Studies I: Phonological and Grammatical Studies in Modern Nahuatl Dialects** by D. F. Robinson et al. (1969) *
20. **The Phonology of Capanahua and its Grammatical Basis** by E. E. Loos (1969) **
21. **Philippine Languages: Discourse, Paragraph and Sentence Structure** by R. E. Longacre (1970) *
22. **Aztec Studies II: Sierra Nahuat Word Structure** by D. F. Robinson (1970) *
23. **Tagmemic and Matrix Linguistics Applied to Selected African Languages** by K. L. Pike (1970) *
24. **A Grammar of Lamani** by R. L. Trail (1970) **
25. **A Linguistic Sketch of Jicaltepec Mixtec** by H. C. Bradley (1970) *
26. **Major Grammatical Patterns of Western Bukidnon Manobo** by R. E. Elkins (1970) *
27. **Central Bontoc: Sentence, Paragraph and Discourse** by L. A. Reid (1970) *
28. **Identification of Participants in Discourse: A Study of Aspects of Form and Meaning in Nomatsiguenga** by M. R. Wise (1971) *
29. **Tupi Studies I** by D. Bendor-Samuel et al. (1971) *
30. **L'Enonce Toura (Côte d'Ivoire)** by R. Bearth (1971) *
31. **Instrumental Articulatory Phonetics: An Introduction to Techniques and Results** by K. C. Keller (1971) *
32. **According to Our ancestors: Folk Texts from Guatemala and Honduras** by M. Shaw et al. (1971) *
33. **Two Studies of the Lancandones of Mexico** by P. Baer and W. R. Merrifield (1971) *
34. **Toward a Generative Grammar of Blackfoot** by D. G. Frantz (1971) *
35. **Languages of the Guianas** by J. E. Grimes et al. (1972) *

36. **Tagmeme Sequences in the English Noun Phrase** by P. Fries (1972) *
37. **Hierarchial Structures in Guajajara** by D. Bendor-Samuel (1972) *
38. **Dialect Intelligibility Testing** by E. Casad (1974) **
39. **Preliminary Grammar of Auca** by M. C. Peeke (1973) *
40. **Clause, Sentence, and Discourse Patterns in Selected Languages of Nepal, parts I, II, III, IV** by A. Hale et al. (1973) **
41. **Patterns in Clause, Sentence, and Discourse in Selected Languages of India and Nepal, parts I, II, III, IV** by R. L. Trail et al. (1973) *
42. **A Generative Syntax of Peñoles Mixtec** by J. Daly (1973) **
43. **Daga Grammar** by E. Murane (1974) *
44. **A Hierarchical Sketch of Mixe as spoken in San José El Paraíso** by W. and J. Van Haitsma (1976) *
45. **Network Grammars** by J. E. Grimes et al. (1975) *
46. **A Description of Hiligaynon Syntax** by E. Wolfenden *
47. **A Grammar of Izi, an Igbo Language** by P. and I. Meier and J. Bendor-Samuel (1975) *
48. **Semantic Relationships of Gahuku Verbs** by E. Deibler (1976) *
49. **Sememic and Grammatical Structures in Gurung** by W. Glover (1974) **
50. **Korean Clause Structure** by Shin Ja Joo Hwang (1976) *
51. **Papers on Discourse** by J. E. Grimes et al. (1978) **
52. **Discourse Grammar: Studies in Indigenous Languages of Colombia, Panama, and Ecuador, parts I, II, III** by R. E. Longacre et al. (1976-77) **
53. **Grammatical Analysis by K. L. and E. G. Pike (1980; revised 1982)   Instructor's Guide for Grammatical Analysis** by K. L. and E. G. Pike (1976) **
54. **Studies in Otomanguean Phonology** by W. R. Merrifield et al. (1977) **
55. **Two Studies in Middle American Comparative Linguistics** by D. Oltrogge and C. Rensch (1977) **
56. **Studies in Uto-Aztecan Grammar, parts I, II, III, IV** by R. W. Langacker et al. (1977-84) **
57. **The Deep Structure of the Sentence in Sara-Ngambay Dialogues** by J. E. Thayer (1978) **
58. **Discourse Studies in Mesoamerican Languages, parts I and II** by L. K. Jones et al. (1979) **
59. **The Functions of Reported Speech in Discourse** by M. L. Larson (1978) **
60. **A Grammatical Description of the Engenni Language** by E. Thomas (1978) **
61. **Predicate and Argument in Rengao Grammar** by K. Gregerson (1979) **
62. **Nung Grammar** by J. E. Saul and N. F. Wilson (1980) **
63. **Discourse Grammar in Ga'dang** by M. R. Walrod (1979) **
64. **A Framework for Discourse Analysis** by W. Pickering (1980) **
65. **A Generative Grammar of Afar** by L. Bliese (1981) **
66. **The Phonology and Morphology of Axininca Campa** by D. L. Payne (1981) **
67. **Pragmatic Aspects of English Text Structure** by L. B. Jones (1983) **
68. **Syntactic Change and Syntactic Reconstruction** by J. R. Costello (1983) **
69. **Affix Positions and Cooccurrences** by J. E. Grimes (1983) **
70. **Babine and Carrier Phonology: A Historically Oriented Study** by G. Story (1984) **
71. **Workbook for Historical Linguistics** by W. P. Lehmann (1984) **
72. **Senoufo Phonology, Discourse to Syllable** by E. Mills (1984) **
73. **Pragmatics in Non-Western Perspective** by G. L. Huttar and K. J. Gregerson (1986) **
74. **English Phonetic Transcription** by Ch.-J. N. Bailey (1985) **
75. **Sentence-initial Devices** by J. E. Grimes et al. (1986) **
76. **Hixkaryana and Linguistic Typology** by D. C. Derbyshire (1985) **

77. **Discourse Features of Korean Narration** by S. J. Hwang (1987) **

78. **Tense/Aspect and the Development of Auxiliaries in Kru Languages** by L. Marchese (1986) **

79. **Modes in Dényá Discourse** by S. N. Abangma (1987) **

For further information or a catalog of all S.I.L. publications write to:

Bookstore
Summer Institute of Linguistics
7500 W. Camp Wisdom Road
Dallas, TX 75236